T0318163

Planning Wild Cities

This book critically engages with the contemporary challenges and opportunities of wild cities in a climate of change.

A key focus of the book is exploring the nexus of possibilities for wild cities and the eco-ethical imagination needed to drive sustainable and resilient urban pathways. Many now have serious doubts about the prospects for humanity to live within cities that are socially just and responsive to planetary limits. Is it possible for planning to better serve, protect, and nurture our human and non-human worlds? This book argues it is.

Drawing on international literature and Australian case examples, this book explores issues around climate change, colonization, urban (in)security, and the rights to the city for both humans and nature. It is within this context that this book focuses on the urgent need to better understand how contemporary cities have changed, and the relational role of planning within it.

Planning Wild Cities will be of particular interest to students and scholars of planning, urban studies, and sustainable development, and for all those invested in reshaping our 'wild' city futures.

Wendy Steele is an Associate Professor in Sustainability and Urban Planning with the Centre for Urban Research at RMIT University, Melbourne Australia. Her research and practice focus on cities in a climate of change, with a particular emphasis on climate justice, urban resilience, critical governance, infrastructures of care and planning theory. Her previous books include *A Climate for Growth*, *Planning Across Borders* and *Global City Challenges: Debating a Concept, Improving a Practice*.

Routledge Research in Sustainable Urbanism

This series offers a forum for original and innovative research that engages with key debates and concepts in the field. Titles within the series range from empirical investigations to theoretical engagements, offering international perspectives and multidisciplinary dialogues across the social sciences.

Imagining Sustainability
Creative Urban Environmental Governance in Chicago and Melbourne
Julie L. Cidell

Regenerative Urban Design and Ecosystem Biomimicry
Maibritt Pedersen Zari

The Politics of Urban Sustainability Transitions
Knowledge, Power and Governance
Edited by Jens Stissing Jensen, Philipp Späth, and Matthew Cashmore

Ecologies Design
Transforming Architecture, Landscape, and Urbanism
Edited by Maibritt Pedersen Zari, Peter Connolly and Mark Southcombe

Planning Wild Cities
Human–Nature Relationships in the Urban Age
Wendy Steele

www.routledge.com/Routledge-Research-in-Sustainable-Urbanism/book-series/RRSU

Planning Wild Cities

Human–Nature Relationships in the Urban Age

Wendy Steele

Routledge
Taylor & Francis Group

LONDON AND NEW YORK

First published 2021
by Routledge
2 Park Square, Milton Park, Abingdon, Oxon OX14 4RN

and by Routledge
605 Third Avenue, New York, NY 10017

First issued in paperback 2022

Routledge is an imprint of the Taylor & Francis Group, an informa business

Publisher's Note
The publisher has gone to great lengths to ensure the quality of this
reprint but points out that some imperfections in the original copies may
be apparent.

British Library Cataloguing-in-Publication Data
A catalogue record for this book is available from the British Library

Library of Congress Cataloging-in-Publication Data
Names: Steele, Wendy, author.
Title: Planning wild cities : human-nature relationships in the
urban age Wendy Steele.
Description: Abingdon, Oxon ; New York, NY : Routledge,
2021. | Series: Routledge research in sustainable urbanism |
Includes bibliographical references and index.
Identifiers: LCCN 2020016698 (print) | LCCN 2020016699
(ebook) | ISBN 9781138917927 (hardback) | ISBN
9781315688756 (ebook)
Subjects: LCSH: City planning–Environmental aspects–Case
studies. | City planning–Social aspects–Case studies. |
Sustainable development–Planning–Case studies.
Classification: LCC HT166 .S6845 2021 (print) | LCC HT166
(ebook) | DDC 307.1/216–dc23
LC record available at https://lccn.loc.gov/2020016698
LC ebook record available at https://lccn.loc.gov/2020016699

ISBN 13: 978-0-367-55157-5 (pbk)
ISBN 13: 978-1-138-91792-7 (hbk)
ISBN 13: 978-1-315-68875-6 (ebk)

DOI: 10.4324/9781315688756

Typeset in Goudy
by Wearset Ltd, Boldon, Tyne and Wear

For
Jesse – sweet child of mine
Russ – the rivers run deep my lover

Contents

Acknowledgements

Context matters. As a Melbourne-based Australian urban scholar I would first like to acknowledge the people of the Woi wurrung and Boon wurrung language groups of the eastern Kulin Nations on whose unceded lands I live and work, and pay my respects to Aboriginal elders, past, present, and emerging. On this Wurundjeri land, Bunjil the eagle is the creator, reminding us of the need to respect, protect, and nurture each other and the land – to care for Country.

I have been very fortunate to have been part of a lively and collegial community of critical scholars whose work has helped shape (and challenge) my thinking around the nature of wild cities over the years. A very special thanks in this regard to Libby Porter, Crystal Legacy, Karyn Bosomworth, Brian Coffey, Lauren Rickards, Jean Hillier, Donna Houston, Diana MacCallum, Jason Byrne, Ilan Wiesel, Cecily Maller, Anitra Nelson, Ian McShane, Yolande Strengers, Aiden Davison, Martin Mulligan, Aviva Reed, Marco Amati, Ben Cooke, Jago Dodson, Brendan Barrett, Karen Hussey, John Handmer, Sarah Pink, Stephen Dovers, Cathy Keys and colleagues in the Centre for Urban Research, RMIT.

This research was funded by an Australian Research Council *Discovery Early Career Researcher Award* (DE120102428). As part of this fellowship I spent a short residence at the University of Newcastle upon Tyne in the UK. My thanks to both Stephen Graham and Simin Davoudi who generously hosted me at the university.

The support I have received from Taylor and Francis Publishing demonstrates that working relationships can be both generous and caring. In the UK, Annabelle Harris and Matthew Shobbrook have been consistently encouraging, kind, and incredibly patient. In Australia, the editorial suggestions and experience of Melanie Scaife were also very constructive and timely.

To my dear, dear friends over many years Jackie Kiewa, Kristen Lyons, Trevor Robertson, and Anthony Esposito, the shared gatherings, breakfasts, and dinners, holidays on remote beaches or walks in the bush and chats over lovely cups of tea. The gentle but persistent question, 'How's the book going?', and prompts to 'open my starry heart', really helped!

To my lovely mum and dad and my three siblings Mike, Katie, and James and their families – so many great adventures together, and so many more to come. Special thanks also to the extended Blamey family for the many enjoyable happy hours and coffee catchups.

My heartlands are at home – this is in Melbourne with Russ and Jesse-man, Scotty, and Anika – each one of us linked by love to the other. We are learning to navigate the wild city together.

Finally, to all in the these strangest and most uncertain of times...

After the Fire (Artist: Melanie Nightingale)[1]

1   Weather of mass destruction

Black summer

We woke to find Australia was on fire. My partner and I peered out from our tent into the red-black gloom, breathing thick, constrained, and wheezy in the fire-thick air. Most other campers had left during the night taking with them their children, bikes, surfboards, dogs, guitars, BBQs, beers, and bravado. With nervous eyes on the wind for any sudden changes, we bundled everything we had into the car and scuttled off into the smoke-filled haze. We were among the tens of thousands of residents and tourists evacuated during Black Summer.

We were the lucky ones.

Across Australia, bushfires ravaged the landscape. Fire tornadoes howled through the day and night. The sky turned black and with it, land, water, and settlements were covered in a thick ash. People lost everything, including their lives, and thousands of homes and businesses were destroyed. Tens of millions of hectares of land were ravaged, and an estimated 1 billion native and domestic animals were burnt alive – their charred remains scattered along the sides of roads where some had tried to seek refuge from the fire. They did not have a chance.

The bushfire danger index registered 'Catastrophic' (the highest rating possible) in many parts of Australia. Some fires were out of control not for days or weeks – but months. In all affected areas the mostly volunteer firefighters battled hot, windy conditions trying to contain the fires. The mood was one of dogged determination, and in some cases, tired resignation. As one fire service volunteer in Victoria explained, 'I looked at my fire brigade captain, who's been doing this for decades, and I could see in his eyes that this was not something we could fight.'[2]

What were we doing in this catastrophic bushfire area? The weather felt adversarial, angry, and unpredictable. It felt like we were all under attack. We, like many, retreated back to the 'safety' of the cities. But the fires came with us. The air quality across Australia that summer was recorded as hazardous, with levels of fine particles in the air categorized as 'very poor' by the Environment Protection Authority. Research shows prolonged exposure to bushfire smoke increases the risk of respiratory illness, smoke-induced stroke, and heart attack, particularly for those most vulnerable such as the elderly. Pregnant women were warned of the dangers of an early miscarriage due to hazardous smoke inhalation.[3] For one day at least, Melbourne was reported as having some of the 'worst air quality in the world'[4] with heightened exposure to small particle toxicity. Trapped in an apartment or house at the end of a cul-de-sac surrounded by smoke-filled air, many people felt claustrophobic. 'Nowhere to run to baby, nowhere to hide'[5] – not even in the urban heartlands of Australia's capital cities.

In previous summers, Russ and I had sea-kayaked together in the Nadgee Wilderness area on the south-eastern Australian coastline. It was blissful to experience this intimate relationship with nature and each other. Nadgee is part of Bidawal, Dthwara, and Monaroo Country, whose people have a long spiritual and cultural association with the area best known for its remote beaches, coastline, lagoons, and dunes. Nadgee Wilderness stretches from the town of Mallacoota in Victoria, to Disaster Bay in New South Wales, named for its shipwreck history. In the past, Nadgee was the perfect counterpoint to home and work in the suburban metropolis: our Christmas holiday rite of wild pilgrimage and passage. But where to go now?

Back in the town of Mallacoota at the edge of the Nadgee Wilderness area, the largest maritime evacuation of Australian citizens in a natural disaster was taking place.[6] With only one road in and one road cut off by fire, more than 4,000 people were stranded at the boat ramp with limited food, fuel, and drinking water. Locals and tourists alike had to be evacuated by navy boats and helicopters. People described the experience as 'mayhem … like Armageddon'.[7]

As the bushfire encircled the now-deserted town of Mallacoota, folk huddled together under a blood-red sky while the houses on the edge of the town burnt. 'Nature has spoken, and she is furious.'[8]

We are the wildfire

In 'Diary of a Wildlife Carer', Rachel Labeter describes her feelings of heartbreak and humility working with endangered and injured animals at the frontline of the Australian bushfire crisis:

We are all responsible for bearing witness to our age ... It is warming up unseasonably of course. In the smoke haze from the bushfires, the mountains are faded water colours ... Grey-headed flying foxes, a vulnerable species, are falling out of trees. Plants aren't flowering and the ones that do bear little pollen or nectar ... Someone tells me that this is just the beginning. I focus on the ash-smudged horizon, determined not to look away ...[9]

The recent bushfires in Australia increased the likelihood of accelerated species extinction, particularly for those species already listed as extremely vulnerable. Unprecedented mass fish die-offs in New South Wales were experienced as heavy rain, washed ash, and charred debris flowed into the rivers after bushfires. In some sections of the Macleay River, thousands of dead, rotting fish were found along 70km of the riverbank, killed by the rapid drops of oxygen levels in the water as a result. As one local resident observes, 'We've seen fish kills on the river after bushfires before, but never anything like this. It will take decades to recover from.'[10]

The World Wildlife Fund (WWF) has set up an urgent appeal across Australia to support koalas who lost up to 30 per cent of their habitat during the bushfires. It estimates nearly 10,000 koalas perished in the fires in New South Wales alone, and 50 per cent of the koala population on Kangaroo Island in South Australia perished. 'Koala populations have declined by a staggering 42 per cent over 20 years and are at serious risk of becoming extinct in NSW and Queensland by 2050. We must act to protect them now, or they could disappear in a matter of decades.'[11]

The toll on native Australian flora and fauna as well as other non-native plant and animal species can only be described as catastrophic (the highest possible rating). Reports estimate more than 1 billion animals died or have been placed in extreme risk because their habitats have been destroyed or they are unable to access food and shelter.[12] Critically endangered species such as the Southern Corroboree frog, the Regent Honeyeater bird, the Western Ground parrot and East Gippsland Galaxias fish all had their habitats further destroyed or severely damaged due to the bushfires, placing their prospects for long-term survival at severe risk.

When a population suffers a series of catastrophic weather events such as bushfires, tornadoes, drought, and floods, we often understand these disasters as 'acts of nature'. Nature in this sense is 'out there', separate from us, capable of unleashing wild weather of mass destruction, which we seek to tame. Maria Kaika argues that the disasters are rarely if ever natural, and almost always related to human politics, activities, and impacts. Nature is not the executor, but the victim of the ways we (mis)manage our relationships with environment.[13]

By laying the blame on 'nature', we hide the devastation on other species, our own role in the disaster and all of the many ways we are complicit to the trauma that ensues. This is a destructive circular relationship as environmentalist Bill McGibbon observes in his book *The End of Nature*.

> If the waves crash up against the beach, eroding dunes and destroying homes, it is not the awesome power of Mother Nature. It is the awesome power of Mother Nature as altered by the awesome power of man, who has overpowered in a century the processes that have been slowly evolving and changing of their own accord since the earth was born.[14]

Putting ourselves back into the picture of natural disasters as disaster protagonists rather than as victims is not easy. Arsonists who purposefully start fires or even thoughtless people who throw out a cigarette butt, which then starts a major bushfire, are castigated, reviled, and even exiled from our community through jail or punishment for the crimes they have committed and the harm they have caused. An aberration of humanity, these people, like nature, are not one of 'us'. Yet how do we account for our everyday roles in warming the planet? We are creating the conditions that lay seed to the disasters such as bushfires, and in doing so we are harming many, including ourselves, our families, and communities.

This is the argument of the Extinction Rebellion global movement, which claims we are in the midst of an extinction of our own making and must act now to halt biodiversity loss and reduce greenhouse gas emissions to net zero by 2025. They call on the state to declare a climate and ecological emergency, and to work with other institutions and community groups to communicate the urgency for change. 'Our main point here is to build a mass movement, to get mainstream people involved in the climate struggle in a way they never have before.'[15]

On Fire, by author Naomi Klein, takes a cue from the popular manifesto put out by British climate strikers: 'Greta Thunberg may have been the spark, but we are the wildfire.'[16] Klein's intention, alongside the strikers, is to highlight the speed with which grassroots climate activism can work to mobilize communities to achieve net zero global carbon emissions. Within the Australian bushfire and national political context, this takes on a very different meaning.

The bushfire impacts to humans and the built infrastructure were only one part of the crisis that unfolded in Australia, including devastating impacts to trees, plants, animals, soil, insects, fish, water, land, and ultimately to the carbon-laden atmosphere itself – and so the cycle goes on. It was not just 'us' that suffered extreme loss during the Black Summer, but all of nature. We are beginning to understand that in the context of anthropogenic or human-induced climate change, it is 'we' who are the fire.

Our house is on fire

'I am here to say, our house is on fire' said student activist and Nobel Peace Prize nominee Greta Thunberg in her address to the World Economic Forum in Davos on 25 January 2019.

I don't want you to be hopeful
I want you to panic
I want you to feel the fear I feel everyday
And then I want you to act
I want you to act as you would in a crisis
I want you to act as if your house is on fire
Because it is.[17]

This is a profound call to arms for urgent global climate action, but also signals the depth of our existential challenge. We are being tasked with putting out the fire that we ourselves have started. Yet we walk backwards with our eyes closed into the growing carbon storm.

'Surviving' was the title of the introduction to the *Griffith Review* in 2011 edited by Julianne Shultz in the context of floods in Queensland and bushfires in Victoria and Western Australia.

The geographic diversity of the island continent means that nature's extremes take different forms, depending on latitude, longitude and patterns of settlement – fires for some, floods and cyclones for others, elsewhere earthquakes and storm surges or the lingering, prodding fingers of drought.[18]

Shultz argued Australia had a new Christmas moniker: the disaster season not the festive season. That was a decade ago.

Little in Australia's engagement with climate change has changed. Public and political awareness is growing that 1) the climate is rapidly changing (i.e. the earth is getting hotter with temperatures rising at an unprecedented rate, causing climate-driven extreme weather events); 2) the impacts will be profound; and 3) we need to take urgent mitigative and adaptive action. However, action on climate change remains ad hoc and low scale across the nation, despite increasingly dire signs that we have entered a 'climate crisis'.

On 7 February 2020, the highest temperature ever recorded for the continent of Antarctica was logged at 18.3°C (64.9°F), which is one of the fastest-warming regions on earth, accelerating the potential for catastrophic sea-level rise.[19] Tasmania's east coast is warming at a rate that is four times the global average, stripping the seabed of its current marine system integrity as tropical water conditions challenge the temperate reef systems.[20] The bushfires in Australia now burn in rainforest, previously too damp for fires to ignite – a key indicator of how dry and dangerous the bushfire conditions are in the current climate of change.[21]

Weather Gone Wild, a report by the Climate Council in Australia, emphasizes that extreme weather events such as bushfires are part of a trend of increasingly frequent catastrophic weather events in Australia and globally. The report highlighted four key findings:

1   The past four years have been the four hottest years on record for global surface temperature, continuing a long-term warming trend.
2   Climate change is increasing the frequency and/or severity of extreme, wild weather both globally and in Australia.
3   The impacts of extreme weather have been damaging and costly.
4   To slow and eventually stop the increase in the frequency and severity of extreme weather, Australia needs an effective national climate policy that drives down greenhouse gas pollution deeply and rapidly as part of a global effort.[22]

Australia now experiences extreme heat, severe bushfires, intense flooding, and drought conditions at the same time. This mirrors recent global events, which included intense hurricanes and wildfires (United States), severe drought (Argentina, South Africa), extreme heat (United Kingdom, Norway, Finland), fires (Greece, Sweden), and extensive storms and/or flooding (Germany, Japan, Indonesia), to name but a few. The compounding impact of multiple events serve to make climate disasters worse: bushfires are intensified by tornadoes, storms, and lightning strikes; landslides are caused when rain hits the charred remains of fire-burnt regions.[23]

The Black Summer bushfires were experienced in every state and territory in Australia, fuelled by a combination of extreme temperatures well over 40 degrees, prolonged periods of drought, and warm winds. For many Australians, the experience of the bushfire disaster was like being in a war-zone. 'A state of emergency' was declared for many states, regional areas, cities, and towns. There were heavy losses of both life and land, and the military and navy were called into evacuate those affected. Crisis centres were set up around Australia with round-the-clock volunteers, and mental health professionals dispatched to assist with the trauma, post trauma, and depression that came along with the disaster – is this the new normal for Australia?

Chief Executive Officer of the Australian Bushfire and Natural Hazards Cooperative Research Centre, Dr Richard Thornton, argues it is, and that the danger of joined-up fires across borders turning in to mega-fires is a key future threat that will exacerbate existing conditions and needs to be much better considered and planned for.

> If you sum up all the fire dangers for each day, that's getting higher over that period as well. Things are getting hotter, they're starting earlier, finishing later, and during the fire season it's a worse fire season than we've seen before. When fires join, we know that period when they're coming together can exacerbate the fire behaviour that you see, so you get much bigger fire behaviour. Once the fires have joined, of course, now you've got a really huge task.[24]

The 'new normal' mantra serves two key purposes. First, it helps *seed the idea* that this is not an unusual or once-in-a-lifetime event, but that the conditions will persist and, if they continue, will become the status quo. Second, the 'new normal' is *a critical provocation* that reminds us that these extreme weather events are generated by anthropogenic climate change, which requires a dramatic reduction in global carbon emissions. The real danger is if the 'new normal' is accepted uncritically and just serves to describe the contemporary climate disaster context, rather than agitating for real change.

The Bloodhound gang's song 'The Roof is on Fire', was the theme to Michael Moore's documentary film *Fahrenheit 9/11*,[25] which focused on 'the depiction of Bush as a lazy and duplicitous leader',[26] mired in complacency and conflicts of interest that President George W. Bush and his inner circle used to exploit the 9/11 attacks to support the power of a corporate and conservative political elite in America.

Australia is one of the most carbon-intensive economies in the world and has signed the Paris Agreement to make a 26–28 per cent reduction in its emissions compared with 2005 levels, by 2030. The weather of mass destruction will not go away. It will continue to manifest with unprecedented speed and intensity. The house is on fire and the heat is rising fast. Despite this, the Australian Government has failed to act in accordance with international agreements, and without action, Australia is unlikely to meet our internationally agreed climate targets in time.

When you look at Australian climate politics, it is not just the weather that is wild.

Lucky country

The questions posed by journalist and social critic Donald Horne about Australian complacency and in-action in *The Lucky Country*[27] are as unsettling today as they were when it was published 50 years ago. Although contemporary Australia has changed in that time, the premise is the same: that the lucky country might not be so lucky. The book was a wake-up call to an anxious, unimaginative, and discontented Australian society.

This is highlighted with prescience with regard to the current climate of crisis and change by politics professor John Keane in his 2010 *Griffith Review* essay entitled 'Out of the Ordinary: Bad luck, Disaster, Democracy', which argues that democracies themselves are not disaster-proof. Propped up as they so often are by property interests, political incompetence and arrogance, and conservative scepticism, democracies can in fact go badly wrong.

> Let us suppose for a moment that Horne was onto something. Imagine that his profound discomfort with the cluelessness of a democracy confronted by big and threatening problems turned out to have global relevance in the twenty-first century. Given that democracies such as Australia are struggling to come to terms with life and death matters such as … climate change and the wilful sabotage of the biosphere, might it be that they are also courting not-yet-known disasters for which they are unprepared?[28]

The bushfires over the Black Summer were not a surprise to scientists and firefighters on the ground. They had warned of the need to prepare for such events, and called for greater funding, training, resources, and infrastructure such as large air tankers able to unleash high volumes of water. The government rejected the proposal for a national fleet of faster air tankers. Back in 2008, economist Ross

Garnaut had warned of the increase in bushfire severity and impact in his review of the impact of climate change on the Australian economy for then prime minister Kevin Rudd. 'Fire seasons will start earlier, and later and be more intense. This effect increases over time but should be directly observable by 2020.'[29]

And so it came to pass in the Black Summer of 2019–20. Relying on bluff and bluster or 'luck' is proving to be entirely inadequate for our climate-challenged times. After months of fighting fires on all fronts, we have been left licking our collective wounds. As communities rebuild and the costs are counted, an increasingly widespread voice for change is inserting itself into the national consciousness and conversation. And perhaps just for once, now that the 'luck' has run dry, mainstream Australia is starting to learn – and to listen.

Indigenous fire management starts with the connection of people to land and to each other; in contemporary Australia this means bringing together a disconnected population with an equally fractured connection to the root and cause of climate-driven disasters. Living in Australia means living on Aboriginal land where people have cared for Country for thousands of years using traditional practices. This is a holistic approach to knowledge, rooted in caring for community and environment as the basis for good fire management.

> Not all white fellas were bad in any era or time, but we can't forget the terrible stories from those old days or the cruel deeds that did happen. It is beyond anyone's mind to understand the damage that has been done to the people and the environment up until this day, and our history is a part of that … Here in Australia the land is suffering more than ever before. The genocide that was cast upon the people is still affecting the country today … This story is just one Aboriginal fire story of many across Australia that are calling people back to country to put the right fire back onto the land. The fire is just the beginning of understanding the important journey ahead for us all.[30]

Instead of blind faith in 'the lucky country', Australians could focus on building connections to Country. This Aboriginal approach to human–nature–culture relations goes to the heart of the fundamental changes required to address climate change-related disasters.

> Country is not a generalized or undifferentiated type of place, such as one might indicate with terms like 'spending a day in the country' or 'going up the country'. Rather, country is a living

entity with a yesterday, today and tomorrow, with a consciousness, and a will toward life. Because of this richness, country is home, and peace; nourishment for body, mind, and spirit; heart's ease.[31]

Victor Steffensen is a descendant of the Tagalaka people on his mother's side in the Gulf Country of Far North Queensland and co-founder of the National Indigenous Fire Workshops. In his book *Fire Country – How Indigenous Fire Management Could Help Save Australia*, he explains 'burning involves identifying what needs to burn from a traditional knowledge perspective' but also 'reconnecting humanity with land and culture again'. He argues that bushfire management is an opportunity for 'healing people with country'.[32] His vision is one of hope that the necessary process of healing in Australia has already begun.

And he is not alone.

Across the country, the work of rebuilding after the summer of disaster has begun, but the work goes far deeper than remaking houses, roads, and infrastructure. There are small seeds of hope that suggest this Black Summer was an opportunity; a tipping point for rethinking and reimagining our relationship to land and each other. We must look further than weather of mass destruction to better understand our own role in this climate of change. 'We need to think carefully and boldly about the sort of place we want Australia to be', observed Julianne Schultz in her editorial 'Still the Lucky Country?' in the *Griffith Review*.[33]

Moving past the lucky country moniker, there is a renewed sense of urgency and opportunity, an opportunity to reinvent the Australian Dream. Cities as our human habitat, and key sites of consumption and production, are a large part of both the problem and the solution. How we plan for and inhabit our cities in the future depends on our understanding of human–nature relations in the urban age. After all, cities would not exist without us.

'The question of the moment is: could we exist without cities?'[34]

Cities in a climate of change

Our cities are now capable of being seen from space: the superstructures of the super-species in the age of the Anthropocene. As home to more than half the world's population, our cities consume nearly three-quarters of the planet's natural resources and are highly vulnerable to the impacts of human-induced climate change.

Important questions around urban food, energy, water, housing, and transport jostle for public and policy attention with ecological imperatives and issues of infrastructure provision and development.

We live in the age of the city. The city is everything to us – it consumes us, and for that reason we glorify it.[35]

We also fear it. Cities for some are 'places of decay, moral turpitude and social disorganization'.[36] For others, such as Chris Abani, the city is 'half slum, half paradise', the writer wondering how they can be so violent, ugly and beautiful at the same time.[37] Whilst Mike Davidson's vision of a 'planet of slums' offers a dystopic image of a twenty-first-century urban world squatting in excrement surrounded by pollution and decay of its own making.[38] The city represents diverse imaginaries for inhabitants and visitors.

To some, it is the centre of civilization, sophistication, wealth, opulence and the haven of the elite. To others, it is the heart of decadence where only the fittest survive, a jungle city of chaos where nothing works but for pickpockets, armed robbers and fraudulent characters.[39]

Like the cities it serves, urban planning is a mirror to humanity – both outcome and response to the urban condition. From its earliest conception, urban planning has sought to correct harms arising from living in cities and to advance a better quality of life for urban residents. As cities became larger and more crowded, growing epidemics of plague and disease afflicted rich and poor alike. 'Shit-and-urine filled they became fertile gardens to feed rats and rat-borne disease.'[40] The purpose of urban and environmental planning was considered to be – at least in part – an instrument of social reform, closely associated with strong reformist ideals around improving human misery and squalor; to create the conditions for 'the good city' to flourish.

That's the positive version anyway.

For some, urban planning is a far more sinister project: a reactive and often regressive response to 'urban land use and development pathology'.[41] The dark side of planning has exposed the underbelly of repressive practices of social control and oppression, which have served at one time or other the vested interests of government agencies, the private sector and community groups alike. There is a restlessness and churning at both the global and local scale where cities serve as the mirror for our contradictions and anxieties.

The history of planning is littered with unintended consequences and undesired outcomes … we are entitled to feel doubtful about the prospects for planning in relation to environmental issues, which arguably constitute some of the most complex problems yet faced by modern societies. This sceptical mood has been reinforced … by the de-legitimation of planning which has accompanied the ascendancy of political perspectives which have poured scorn on the capacities of public agencies to intervene wisely and effectively.[42]

For others, the central question for urban planning should be, 'what kind of role planning can play in developing the city and region within the constraints of a capitalist economy and a democratic system'.[43] Australian planning professor Leonie Sandercock, in her seminal meditation on property, politics, power, and urban planning in *Cities for Sale*, argues that this constitutes a series of complex dilemmas for capitalist democracies around questions such as

whether popular immediate solutions to planning problems are to be preferred to long term more expert ones, whether a combination of popular movements and representative institutions can outweigh entrenched power groups, and whether more participatory and redistributive policies will in the end enhance overall human welfare.[44]

In the twenty-first century, for urban and environmental planners seeking to support sustainability-led change, the task ahead is complex, turbulent, and unclear. The positioning of planning as a whipping post for society's discontents is well rehearsed, yet few envisage an urban world *sans* planning. Many have serious doubts about the prospects for planning, but what of its potential for helping us to live within our ecological and planetary limits? Is it possible for planning to better serve, protect, and nurture our human and non-human worlds?

This book argues it is.

The aim of this book is to critically engage with the contemporary challenges of planning wild cities in a climate of change. Key issues around urban (in)security, critical infrastructure and the rights to the city for both humans and nature are highlighted. Fundamentally, it is about reframing our relationship with nature. It is within this context that the need to better understand the progressive potential of both contemporary cities and planning is reinforced. This is the provocation of the *Wild City*.

If we are the wildfire, what are we going to do about it?

This introductory chapter, 'Weather of Mass Destruction', has set out both the provocation and framework for the book's structure and content. The focus on Australia's Black Summer highlights not just the vulnerability of the natural landscape but 'the precarity of urban life in the face of climate-induced disasters'.[45] These impacts are not generated by a vengeful nature 'out there', but by the consumption and complacency of us who live 'in here'. We cannot simply retreat back to our lifeboat cities. Instead, like the zombie apocalypse movie *Get Out*, the wild weather, wild capitalism, wild people, and wild politics will all still be waiting for us in the urban shadows – in our habitats and homes – in the cities and settlements we created.

In Australia, we have demonstrated we have the capacity to generate the emissions that are contributing to global warming and causing climate-fuelled catastrophes and disasters. We have yet to demonstrate we can make the scale of changes required at speed for humanity to continue to exist – by repurposing our current systems towards radically reducing our carbon footprint. Part of this entails giving substance to notions such as equity and justice and our ethical attempts to craft the way we collectively live. How can we better shape the conditions of our cities within the context of climate change? What kind of urban futures are we planning?

In Chapter 2, 'Finding Homo Urbanis', the focus simultaneously turns inwards and outwards to grapple with the role of the urban age in this current climate of crisis and change. Within the major cities – where the majority of people live – the immediacy and potentially catastrophic nature of climate risks pose challenges to democracy and governance. Is this the end of cities (as we know it)? For global economists such as Ed Glaeser, the 'triumphant city' has conquered,[46] whilst others see hope in the lifeboat qualities and capacities of cities that will help to navigate the impending urban storm.[47]

Our cities lie at the nexus between the past, present, and future and must be understood in context. Culturally, geographically, and spatially specific, cities have a context – a global context unbound with investment, technology, and a footprint that extends beyond jurisdictional or administrative borders, but also unique cultural landscapes and settlement trajectories. 'We are still settling Australia',[48] and this continues today on the genocide of unceded Aboriginal land. How do we care for urban 'Country'?

'Through the Security Glass Darkly' is the focus of Chapter 3, which explores what happens when urban planning fails. Urban society's vulnerability depends on 'critical nodes' that comprise the critical infrastructure system in key areas such as energy, food, communications, and water. The interdependent nature of cities makes critical urban infrastructure more vulnerable to external impacts, where a disturbance rapidly affects different sectors. Infrastructure networks are often invisible in cities, 'the forgotten, the background, the frozen in place'.[49]

Chapter 4, 'Seeking the Good City' turns the spotlight on the urban age as a quest for the 'good life' and human flourishment. In particular, does the premise of 'the good' city need to be re-thought or at least critically reflected on in the context of climate change? Good for whom – the poor, the earth, non-humans? Good when – now, in the past, in the future, in our imagination? Good by whose standards – the wealthy, the technocrats? Notions of the city and citizens are grounded in what it means to be human, and articulated by 'good city' ideals.

Chapter 5, 'We are the Wild City', builds on this to engage with the potential for living within our limits in the city. Despite our attempts to break down and transcend the divide between the human and non-human, the urban wilds remain negatively, passively, or weakly imagined in visions of possible urban civilisation and futures. To address this will require a more thoroughly problematic glimpse of ourselves, past, present, and future – to politically re-discover and re-engage with *the urban nature* of our wild cities and ourselves.

Chapter 6 centres on a vision for 'Planning *in* Climate Change'. This involves articulating ways to develop urban planning as a collective project through which to navigate climate change. The planning project, whilst full of frustrations and contradictions, is most effective when it focuses on 'what it takes to act in the world to pursue *collective purposes* in ways which attend to the significance of the spatial dimension of all relations and to the particularities of place qualities as they evolve'.[50] The planning response envisaged is one that seeks to build a different kind of city and a different kind of urbanisation.

The final Chapter 7 explores the question, can the wild city be tamed? Is it possible for urban planning to better serve, protect and nurture both our human and more-than-human worlds? What opportunities for those most vulnerable would unfold if planning was framed at heart as a focus on people, values, and ethics, and a commitment to working with, not against, nature? What would our cities be like then?

'Our house is on fire', climate activist Greta Thunberg insists, 'We are facing a disaster of unspoken sufferings for enormous amounts of people … and on climate change we have failed … but we can still fix this.'[51] The challenge, however, is enormous as indicated on the Australian Broadcasting Corporation's 'Q+A' special programme on the Australian bushfires:

The rivers have stopped running
The rain is no longer coming
And now the land is burning ...[52]

An important starting point is the cities, where many now argue 'the battle against climate change will be won or lost'.[53] There is no doubt we are in a 'climate emergency' as the evidence is all around us. However, we must start by reframing human–nature relations and the ways in which we live. To do this requires understanding the impact and possibilities of ourselves and our habitats in this urban age. We must journey into the wild.

Notes

1 Vale Melanie Nightingale (2018) Artist, Entrepreneur, Dear Friend, you are remembered and very much missed.

2 Morton, R (2019) 'The Long, Hot Summer', *The Saturday Paper*, 21 December 2019–24 January 2020, No. 284, available on www.thesaturdaypaper.com.au

3 Robertson, S and Hull L (2020) 'Pregnant Women Should Take Extra Care to Minimise Their Exposure to Bushfire Smoke', *The Conversation*, January, accessed on https://theconversation.com/pregnant-women-should-take-extra-care-to-minimise-their-exposure-to-bushfire-smoke-

4 *The Guardian* (2020) 'Melbourne's Air Quality "Worst in the world" as Bushfires Continue to Burn across Victoria', 14 January, www.theguardian.com/australia-news/2020/jan/14/melbourne-choked-by-hazardous-smoke-as-bushfires-continue-to-burn-across-victoria

5 Adapted from Martha and the Vandellas (1985) 'Nowhere to Run' on the Dance Party album.

6 Koob, S (2020) ' "Like Times of War": Inside the Huge Mallacoota Evacuation', 10 January, accessed on www.theage.com.au/national/victoria/like-times-of-war-inside-the-huge-mallacoota-evacuation-20200110-p53qdr.html

7 Davidson, H (2019) 'Mallacoota Fire: Images of "Mayhem" and "Armageddon" as Bushfires Rages', *The Guardian*, 31 December, accessed on www.theguardian.com/australia-news/2019/dec/31/mallacoota-fire-mayhem-armageddon-bushfires-rage-victoria-east-gippsland

8 O'Malley, M (2020) 'On the Beach in Mallacoota', *Sydney Morning Herald*, 26 January, accessed on www.smh.com.au/national/koalas-shrieked-as-they-burnt-on-the-beach-in-mallacoota-20200106-p53p4a.html

9 Labeter, R (2019) 'Diary of a Wildlife Carer', *The Saturday Paper*, No. 284, 21 December–24 January, pp. 36–7. This essay was the winner of the Horne Prize for non-fiction 2019 (www.thehorneprize.com.au/news)

10 Gair, K (2020) 'Bushfires: "Ecological disaster" ', *The Australian*, 16 January, accessed on www.theaustralian.com.au/science/bushfires-ecological-disaster-as-mass-fish-kill-stretches-70km/news-story/24a0b7110755e106bfc359c09991f7d7

11 WWF (2020) 'Bushfire Emergency – Adopt a Koala', accessed on https://donate.wwf.org.au/adopt/koala?t=AD1920O01&f=41140-227&gclid=EAI

aIQobChMIupX-lOHF5wIVQbaWCh0TnQcGEAAYASAAEgJiSfD_BwE #gs.wiu6kj

12 Scarr, S, Sharma, M., and Hernandez, M (2020) 'Assessing Australia's Ecological Disaster', Reuters, 21 January, accessed on https://graphics.reuters.com/AUSTRALIA-BUSHFIRES-WILDLIFE/0100B5672VM/index.html

13 Kaika, M (2019) 'Political Ecology', accessed on www.youtube.com/watch?v=Z5PRfxNUBao

14 McGibbon, B (1989) *The End of Nature*, Penguin, London.

15 ABC (2019) 'Extinction Rebellion Strains Police Resources', accessed on www.abc.net.au/news/2019-10-13/extinction-rebellion-protests-disrupt-melburne-cost-thousands/11598086

16 Klein, N (2019) *On Fire: The Burning Case for a Green New Deal*, Penguin, London.

17 Thunberg, G (2019) *No One is Too Small to Make a Difference*, Penguin, London.

18 Schultz, J (2011) 'Life in a Time of Disasters', in *Surviving, Griffith Review*, 35, Griffith University, pp. 7–11.

19 Readfern, G (2020) 'Antarctica Logs Hottest Temperature on Record with a Reading of 18.3C', *The Guardian*, 7 February, accessed on www.theguardian.com/world/2020/feb/07/antarctica-logs-hottest-temperature-on-record-with-a-reading-of-183c

20 Hosier, P (2020) 'These Waters off Tasmania's East Coast are Warming Up', ABC News, 10 February, accessed on www.abc.net.au/news/2020-02-08/tasmania-east-coast-warming-four-times-global-average/11889628

21 Lloyd, S (2019) 'Can Rainforest Burn?' ABC News, 10 September, accessed on www.abc.net.au/news/2019-09-09/gold-coast-hinterland-bushfire-why-rainforests-burn/11491364

22 Steffen, W, Dean, A, and Rice, M (2019) 'Weather Gone Wild: Climate Change Fuelled Extreme Weather', Climate Council of Australia, accessed on www.climatecouncil.org.au/wp-content/uploads/2019/02/Climate-council-extreme-weather-report.pdf

23 Hao Z, Singh VP. and Hao F (2017) 'Compound Extremes in Hydroclimatology: A Review', *Water*, 10(6): 1–24, Kopp RE, Hayhoe K, Easterling DR, Hall T, Horton R, Kunkel KE, and LeGrande AN (2017) 'Potential Surprises – Compound Extremes and Tipping Elements', in *Climate Science Special Report: Fourth National Climate Assessment*, Vol. I, Wuebbles, DJ, Fahey, DW, Hibbard, KA, Dokken, DJ, Stewart, BC, and Maycock, TK (eds), U.S. Global Change Research Program, Washington, DC, USA: 411–29.

24 Thornton, R (2020) 'Australian Bushfires – Is This the New Normal?', 3AW News Talk, 3 January, accessed on www.3aw.com.au/the-new-normal-bushfire-expert-weighs-in-on-the-inferno-gripping-australia/

25 *Fahrenheit 9/11* is a documentary film directed by Michael Moore and was released in 2004.

26 Shenan, P (2004) 'In Fahrenheit 9/11 What Are the Facts?' *Chicago Tribunal*, accessed on www.chicagotribune.com/lifestyles/chi-0406200376jun20-story.html

27 Horne, D (2008) *The Lucky Country*, Penguin, London (first published in 1964).

28 Keane, J (2010) 'Out of the Ordinary: Bad Luck, Disaster, Democracy', *Griffith Review*, 28: 210.

29 Garnaut, R. (2008) *The Garnaut Climate Change Review – Final Report.* Cambridge University Press, Melbourne.

30 Steffensen, V (2020) *Fire Country: How Indigenous Fire Management Could Help Save Australia,* Hardie Grant Publishing, Melbourne.

31 Bird Rose, D (1996) *Nourishing Terrains.* Australian Heritage Commission, Canberra.

32 Steffensen, V (2020) *Fire Country: How Indigenous Fire Management Could Help Save Australia,* Hardie Grant Publishing, Melbourne.

33 Schultz, J (2010) 'Cashing in the Chips, in *Still the Lucky Country.'* *Griffith Review* 28: 11.

34 Reader, J (2004) *Cities,* Vintage, London.

35 Okome, O (2002) 'Writing the Anxious City', in O Enwezor *et al.* (eds), *Under Siege: Four African Cities – Freetown Johannesburg,* Ostfildern-Ruit, Kinshasa.

36 Beauregard, R (2003) *Voices of Decline: Post-war Fate of U.S Cities,* Routledge, New York.

37 Abani, C (2004) *Graceland,* Grove Press, New York.

38 Davis, M (2006) *Planet of Slums,* Verso, London.

39 Harrison, S (2012) ' "Suspended City": Personal, Urban, and National Development in Chris Abani's Graceland', *Research in African Literatures,* 43(2): 95–114.

40 Sennett, R (2018) *The Craftsman,* Yale University Press, New Haven, p. 21.

41 Dear, M and Scott, A (1981) *Urbanization and Urban Planning in Capitalist Society,* Methuen, New York.

42 Kenny, M and Meadowcroft, J (1999) *Planning Sustainability,* Routledge, London, p. 1.

43 Campbell, S and Fainstein, S (eds) (2005) *Readings in Planning Theory,* Blackwell, Oxford, p. 1.

44 Sandercock, L (1975) *Cities for Sale: Property, Politics and Urban Planning in Australia,* Melbourne University Press, Melbourne, p. 46.

45 Dawson, A (2017) *Extreme Cities: The Peril and Promise of Urban Life in the Age of Climate Change,* Verso, London, p. 5.

46 Glaeser, E (2011) *Triumph of the City,* Penguin, New York.

47 Gleeson, B (2010) *Lifeboat Cities,* UNSW Press, Sydney.

48 Dovers, S (2000) *Still Settling Australia: Environment, History, and Policy,* Oxford University Press, Oxford.

49 Graham, S (2010) *Disrupted Cities: When Infrastructure fails,* Routledge, New York, p. 10.

50 Healey, P (2007) *Urban Complexity and Spatial Strategies: Towards a Relational Planning for Our Times,* Routledge, New York, p. xi.

51 Thunberg, G (2020) *No One is Too Small to Make a Difference,* Penguin Books, London, p. 18.

52 Woman 2 (2020) 'Q + A Bushfire Special', ABC, Melbourne, accessed on www.abc.net.au/qanda/2020-03-02/11906192

53 Suliman, A (2018) *Climate Battle Will be Won or Lost in Cities, Says UN Climate Chief,* Reuters, accessed on www.reuters.com/article/us-climatechange-un-cities/climate-battle-will-be-won-or-lost-in-cities-says-un-climate-chief-idUSKBN1HX2QI

The Climbers (Artist: Michael Steele)

2   Finding *Homo urbanis*

5D movies on speed

We shape the city and it shapes us. The city as shapeshifter poses a
genuine conundrum for those who seek urban change to address the
climate emergency. Like a 5D movie on speed, the contemporary
city defies conventional boundaries. The BBC series *City in the Sky*
focuses our attention on the sheer number of people who travel in
the air and the extent of the infrastructure built up to support them.
'At any one time there are a million people flying above our heads.
But what does it take to run this city in the sky?'[1] This aerial citizenry is due to double in the next 20 years and with it the global networks, smart technology, and urban infrastructure that make it all
possible – not to mention the increasing carbon emissions, which by
2050 are expected to take up almost a quarter of the available global
carbon budget.[2]

The provocation of the city in the sky is not just making more
visible the impact of urban worlds that exist above the earth and
below – in the sky, land, or sea – critical as this is. It is also a wake-up
call for the need for us to better understand both the complex nature
and make-up of our habitats, and our own deeply conflicted and paradoxical role within it.

Cities are both outcome and agent of human progress, and act as
the sites for the contradictions and anxieties of *Homo urbanis*. They
serve as a mirror for our dreams, ambitions, and discontents. This
raises new questions about what we imagine 'the city' to be, who is
involved, and how we can shape them differently into the future.
Celebrated Australian artist Brett Whiteley reflects this tumultuous
creativity and sensuality in his Sydney Harbour-based paintings, such
as *Self-portrait in the Studio* (1976).

'Self-portrait in the studio' exudes a sense of sumptuous living and the liquid presence of the harbour through what he called the ecstasy-like effect of Ultramarine blue. However, this painting also hints at a darker side, as Wendy Whiteley explained in 1995: 'He was warning himself and other people watching. It was the cage of his interior, his addiction, the window or a glimpse of possible escape into paradise: the escape from one's psyche.'[3]

The challenge for our cities in a climate- and energy-constrained future is to recognize the trajectories of settlement history, and the specificities of governance, policy, and planning in context. The New Urban Agenda adopted in 2016 at the United Nations Conference in Quito, Ecuador, supports this and argues a better, more sustainable future involves a shared vision around cities and urbanization processes.

A new urban agenda for the 21st century recognises the ever-changing dynamics of human civilisation.[4]

The population of Australia, for example, is set to grow to 36 million in the next 30 years, leading political, policy, and public attention to focus on what this means for the future of Australian cities amidst the speed, magnitude, and complexity of change. Despite all the advances that have occurred in technology, the arts, architecture, design and the sciences, there is surprisingly little innovation, even discussion about what might be possible for twenty-first-century Australian settlements beyond the remit of the capital cities. Put simply, are we thinking too narrowly when we talk about cities?

A nation of cities

Australia's future cities lie at the nexus between the past, present, and future, and must be understood in context. For Australian cities located precariously on the coastline, with the majority of the population located in the five large capital cities, the climate and energy challenges take on a particular poignancy and urgency. Culturally, geographically, and spatially specific, Australian cities have a context: a global context unbound with investment, technology and a footprint that extends beyond jurisdictional or administrative borders, but also a rich local context, albeit grounded in the unresolved history of unceded Aboriginal land.

Always was, always will be, Aboriginal land.

Early Australian cities were colonial settlements established by the genocide and stolen land of Aboriginal people who had lived on and cared for the land for millennia. Approximately 400 Aboriginal nations were already in existence when the colonialists arrived in the 1700s and determined the land was *terra nullius* (no one's land). Nothing could be further from the truth. As violent as it was prejudiced, Aboriginal genocide was based on settler-colonial racism, which framed Aboriginal people as a type of 'sullen wilderness, that demands to be subdued and civilized'.[5] This is not just history. 'Indigenous communities in Australia continue to struggle with incarceration, homelessness, and dislocation from history and heritage.'[6]

Always was, always will be, Aboriginal land.

Urban planning professor Libby Porter highlights how Australia as an urban country – a nation of cities – is also urban *Country*.

All places in Australia are indigenous places. Every inch of glass, steel, concrete and tarmac is dug into and bolted onto, Country. Every place that is the subject of analysis and urban intervention is knitted into the fabric of indigenous law and sociality. Country is everywhere.[7]

References to this day in white Australia to 'wilderness areas' such as the desert as being 'untouched', reinforce a remarkable blindness and cruel disrespect to Aboriginal people who have cared for Country for thousands of years. As Jenny Munro of the Wiradjuri nation explains:

From time immemorial, we believe as Aboriginal people, Australia has been here from the first sunrise, our people have been here along with the continent, with the first sunrise. We know our land was given to us by Baiami, we have a sacred duty to protect that land, we have a sacred duty to protect all the animals that we have an affiliation with through our totem system.[8]

Within just a few hundred years, white 'civilization' has eroded and degraded Country including the sky, sea, lands and inland waterways, and introduced exotic species such as cats, foxes, and rabbits. Farming and development practices have led to the destruction of habitats and subsequent extinction of native species, such as the desert rat kangaroo, two kinds of bandicoot, four varieties of wallaby, and the dusky flying fox, at the highest rate of anywhere in the world. Since colonization, it is estimated that 30 out of 273 native animals on the continent have become extinct; this is a rate of one to two extinctions a year.[9] This in turn has global implications.

If such high rates of extinction of mammals are condoned in Australia, there may be little hope for the world's biodiversity more generally.[10]

Built on the appropriation of Aboriginal land, the early (colonial) cities in Australia were defined by distance and isolation – from the rest of the world, and from each other. They hugged the coastline, looking out to sea, fixated on the wealth and importance of trade that linked these cities back to the English motherland. As historian Geoffrey Blainey describes, Australian cities 'stood like [white] seagulls on the sea-cliffs', as they do today.[11]

The sea, not the land, was the primary mode of transport, with a spine of mountains along the east coast of the nation impeding transport development across states and making internal migration of the colonial population difficult. There were no canals and rivers offering carriageway across the nation, as was the case in the United States. The population gravitated to the handful of major cities – just as they do today.

> White Australians established themselves at a few convenient seaports around the endless coastline, hurled themselves against the intimidating interior and retired baffled, broken and defeated to their starting points … they clustered into half a dozen booming, bustling coastal cities in a manner which seemed incomprehensible, almost immoral to other societies … the abnormal aggregation of the population in their capital cities is a most unfortunate element of the progress of the colonies … the concentration of the mass of people in a few large cities is anything but conducive to public health, morality or happiness … but the ignorant brutes will *not* leave the cities, everywhere the monster of urbanism is bursting its chains.[12]

By the 1970s, Australian cities hummed with development as foreign investment generated 'eddies of money'. Journalist and social critic Donald Horne called this *The Time of Hope*.[13] As the Australian mega-city regions began to emerge around the capital cities, a pearl necklace of cities stretched along the eastern coastline from Townsville in Queensland, through to Geelong in Victoria. Cities became massive urban conglomerations, and the problems of sprawl and expansionism were exacerbated with the post-war years.

Indigenous Australian writer Tony Birch makes this personal in this excerpt from his account of the urbanization of Melbourne.

> ...government came up with the idea to build a new freeway, beginning outside my front gate, stretching into the leafy eastern suburbs. It was a plan that would destroy country. The freeway, planned to abut *my* river, would consist of five lanes in each direction, a utopian solution that would put an end to one of Melbourne's most congested traffic locations ... It would be only a short time after the opening of the Eastern Freeway that the state's most recent super artery, opened to allow the city to breathe, would clog the city's veins yet again ... a city that has undergone more than one quadruple bypass which is yet to save the patient.[14]

For Australian cities, love has come too late, if ever.

Finding new ways to transition from the built environment of British colonialism to the new urban spaces required for sustainable futures, including new modes and patterns of urban development, was a key theme in the work of Australian cities advocate Patrick Troy. This includes how to accommodate diverse and changing urban activities, as well as provide and finance urban services. His plea was that the answer would not be found in physical or technological determinism alone, but must be understood in concert with changing political, economic, and social forces. Together, these factors shape the planning of cities and the distribution of resources within them.

> Because cities are the places where most people live, where most goods and services are produced and traded and because they are the primary sources of advanced technology and business innovation, what happens in them and to them is of central importance to society. The better they are planned and developed, the more effective they can be. Their structure, nature and function affects the quality of life, social justice, equity and the natural environment.[15]

The Grattan Institute's 2015 report *City Limits – Why Australia's Cities are Broken and How Can We Fix Them* argues that 'for most of the twentieth century, our cities gave us some of the highest living standards in the world. But they are no longer keeping up with changes in how we live and how our economy works.' Examples cited are the lack of housing affordability, increasing commute times, rising living costs and a growing divide between the rich and poor.

Neglecting our cities has real consequences for our lives now, and for our future prosperity.[16]

Our ideas around Australian cities are changing, yet the processes that shape the change in our cities are not well understood. It is further complicated if notions of what constitutes 'the city' are constrained and outdated. We are now seeing an almost seamless link-up of cities and towns into complex mega-metropolitan regions. 'There is a sense that a high income is not enough to lead a good life – a continuously rising income is needed. Coupled with the high inequality in society and a worsening environmental footprint, it all points to threats to the sustainability of our current standard of living.'[17]

Within this new urban order, planning and managing this metropolitan complexity is crucial. This requires imagination. But in Australia, it has been characterized by a lack of institutional co-ordination and policy integration. A spatial settlement inversion/invasion has taken place. What were previously urban islands along the coastline of Australia are now interconnected, linear urban corridors. Natural and agricultural islands are left adrift in an ever-growing urban landscape. Green space now forms the island amidst a sea of urban sprawl and development.

These emerging Australian mega-metro regions have uneven and inequitable spatial settlement patterns, increasing levels of diseconomies of scale. This is significant, particularly in terms of further exacerbating existing deficits in core public services, water resources, agricultural land, and ecological integrity across jurisdictional borders. The messy reality of colliding urban settlements is that they do not adhere neatly to local, regional, or state administrative boundaries.

Relying on parallel multi-level governance mechanisms that are institutionally divided will not address the issues and challenges we see in cities at the mega-metro scale. The resulting impact affects the ecological and economic capacity of these vast urban corridors, as well as the overall quality of life of those who live within them.

Governing a mega-metro region involves all three tiers of government (local, state, national). It also takes input from the private and community sectors working together. There is currently neither the power nor influence at any single level of government to tackle broader metro-wide concerns around public transport, water security, energy, sewerage and public housing. Meanwhile, the problems of rising infrastructure demands, socio-spatial inequities and issues of ecological integrity intensify and fester in the borderlands of these colliding cities.

Within our lifetime, we could see one long linear conurbation along the length of the eastern coastline of Australia – the rise of the coastal megalopolis. Whether this is desirable or sustainable should be the focus of robust planning and public deliberation. We need to discuss decentralized urban concentration. It should not be left to a default position that emphasizes stand-alone Australian cities that – in terms of growth and development – have already slipped their metro moorings and started to sail away.

How to better plan and manage our cities and urban regions is the contemporary challenge. This requires understanding the role and nature of our cities in climate change, and the forces that shape them, including ourselves. Understanding the 'basic conceptions and images of urban life and urban structure are extraordinarily important, since they often shape the ends envisioned, and the means by which those ends are implemented, by those intent on reinforcing or remaking the existing urban scene'.[18] As Australian geographer Clive Forster in *Australian Cities: Continuity and Change* emphasizes, 'Any visions of radically different cities in the future have to start from here.'

A fairer, more sustainable future for Australian cities beckons.

The angel of (urban) history

There is no document of civilisation which is not at the same time a document of barbarism.

These are the words of German Jewish writer Walter Benjamin, written just before his suicide after the Nazis' invasion of France, and which are inscribed on his gravestone. The words are taken from his work on *Theses on the Philosophy of History*. Benjamin lived in a climate of political change and argued then, that 'the tradition of the oppressed teaches us that the "state of emergency" in which we live is not the exception but the rule'. Benjamin wrote perhaps his most enduring and powerful allegory about the 'angel of history'.

This is how one pictures the angel of history. His face is turned toward the past. Where we perceive a chain of events, he sees one single catastrophe which keeps piling wreckage and hurls it in front of his feet. The angel would like to stay, awaken the dead, and make whole what has been smashed. But a storm is blowing in from Paradise; it has got caught in his wings with such a violence that the angel can no longer close them. The storm irresistibly propels him into the future to which his back is turned, while the pile of debris before him grows skyward. This storm is what we call progress.[19]

The writing is based on a painting by Paul Klee named *Angelus Novus,* which shows an angel staring wide-eyed out of the picture directly at us. Hands in the air, mouth and nostrils open, the throat exposed. Some have argued Benjamin offers 'a melancholy view of historical process as an unceasing cycle of despair'.[20] Humanity is depicted as being trapped in a cycle of self-made destruction – impotent and in limbo between conditions of catastrophe and hope; desperately wanting to run, but seemingly unable to move or look away.

Benjamin himself wrote that

what drives men and women to revolt against injustice is not dreams of liberated grandchildren, but memories of enslaved ancestors. It is by turning our gaze to the horrors of the past, in the hope that we will not thereby be turned to stone, that we are impelled to move forward.[21]

The 'Angel of Alternate History' is a contemporary take on Benjamin's vision of *Angelus Novus* within the contemporary climate of political, environmental, and social change by writer Rebecca Solnit. Her book *Hope in the Dark* offers a counter-narrative. The angel of history says, 'Terrible,' but this angel says, 'Could be worse.' They are both right, but the latter angel gives us grounds to act.[22] This is instructive when we think about our cities.

The Western response to the question 'what is a city?' is closely linked to the question 'what is a human?' Both have many possible responses that emerge from notions of settlement and civilization. Part of the culture and technology associated with us as *Homo sapiens* separate from other species revolves around our capacity to create tools, fire, clothing, and art. The dwelling space as a form of territorial claim can be seen in other species, but the use of technology such as tools to modify the habitat environment is unique to the history of the human species. Caves, rock shelters, simple structures, living sites[23] – these are a uniquely human phenomenon, and a socio-techno modification process that continues to this day.

In the West, early hamlets and villages paved the way for what were to become the first cities. Three characteristics identified the newly emerging cities: a purposeful shift away from the land and nature; an increase in the size, nature and complexity of community within each city; and attempts to achieve order over nature. This was a dramatic shift in the form of human settlements – using economies of scale to build power and influence over the hinterland through the cities and to demarcate where nature ends and the civilized human starts.[24] But there is a double-edged sword, as the colonial-settler literature shows us.

> Settlement or more sharply invasion, is given material presence and organizational shape through processes of urbanisation … the racist imaginaries deployed by colonizers of indigenous peoples has worked to render the urban as a place not indigenous … Cities as sites and symbols of the profound displacement, erasure and often destruction of Indigenous histories and geographies and are at the same time precisely the form that keeps that displacement hidden.[25]

The emergence of the 'walled city', for example, was designed as much to protect the city and keep the inhabitants in, as keep the unwanted out, whether it be humans or animals. The cycle of walled empire thus worked both *outwards* in the seizure of new people and lands, and *inwards* through urban control and regulation of polity.[26] This was achieved through voluntary agreement and mutual cooperation, or through coercion, intimidation, and violence.

Urbanist Lewis Mumford describes the latter city as 'a container of disruptive internal forces, directed towards ceaseless destruction and extermination'. The metaphor of the 'bursting container' was intended as a critique of the expansion of urban life into a powerful megalopolis 'suppressing or destroying the organic tissue of community'.[27] The dramatic end point for Mumford is the 'necropolis' or city of the dead.

> Each historic civilization begins with a living urban core, the polis, and ends in a common graveyard of dust and bones, a Necropolis or city of the dead: fire scorched ruins, shattered buildings, empty workshops, heaps of meaningless refuse, the population massacred or driven into slavery.[28]

Author Isaac Asimov's giant sci-fi planet of Trantor, with a population of 45 billion people focused almost entirely on administration of the planet, has been used by French philosopher and urbanist Henri Lefebvre as a metaphor for future urban living. Trantor was a single planet-city and seat of the imperial authority of the Galactic Empire.

The fall of the Galactic Empire and demise of Trantor is modelled on the fate of the Roman Empire, as the centralized nature of power is increasingly challenged by the periphery. At its peak, the Galactic Empire was made up of almost 25 million planets settled exclusively by humans across the Milky Way. According to the fictional Encyclopedia Galactica, Trantor was:

> ... the centre of the Imperial Government for unbroken hundreds of generations and located, as it was, toward the central regions of the Galaxy among the most densely populated and industrially advanced worlds of the system, it could scarcely help being the densest and richest clot of humanity the Race had ever seen.

Twenty separate agricultural worlds supported the urbanized planet of *Trantor*. This dependence for food on the outer planets made Trantor increasingly vulnerable, despite initial efforts to be self-sufficient through micro-farms and other initiatives. This is uncomfortably close to current reports on the state of the global environment. The Global Footprint Calculations based on United Nations data tells us that if we want to 'continue living as we do without making any changes ... we'll have to find three to four more Earths to support us'.

This is not science-fiction – it is real. Taken to its extreme, the whole earth becomes one city like Trantor – one might imagine the Star Wars Death Star – devoid of the natural world and wholly reliant on technology and other worlds to sustain our ever-increasing population and needs.

A different way of thinking about this is to try to focus on 'what is *not* a city'. This could be based on scale (e.g. a farm, a fishing village, an eco-lodge, a military base) or perhaps be a clear natural contrast to the built environment (i.e. nature, wilderness, the sea, the countryside). The implication is that cities are a concentration of the 'built' environment (i.e. buildings, roads, services, houses etc.), which can be clearly bounded and identified.

Economies of scale and separation from nature were central features of the early cities. This is problematic, however: what if a river runs through the city? What about greenspace in cities? Where does urbanization stop, and non-urbanized landscapes start? As Mumford predicted, 'A city is symbolically a world; and the world in practice is now a city.'[29]

For French philosopher Henri Lefebvre, the narrow definition of 'the city' should be replaced by the broader concept of 'urban

society'. He argues this would shift the way we understand human settlement ambition and expansion as process rather than simply
outcome.[30] Through the lens of 'the urban', the idea of the city as a
'bounded container' gives way to ideas of the city of flow, capital and
mobility. The urban becomes less a 'walled city' and more about
'encounters in space, a dense and differential social space ... filled by a
certain notion of proximity, by people and activity, by events coming
together in this proximity, creating concentration and simultaneity, as
well as density and intensity'.[31]

Just what constitutes 'the urban', however, is not straightforward,
and unpacking this further is taken up as a critical provocation by
urban geographers Neil Brenner and Christian Schmidt from the
Harvard Theory Lab. They draw attention to the emergence of new
socio-spatial reconfigurations, which they argue are reshaping the way
we understand human activity on earth. This 'planetary urbanization'
includes the creation of new 'urban galaxies' of metropolitan regions
that transcend national and state boundaries, and the blurring and re-
articulation of urban territories such as the Aeropolis. It also signifies
the end of 'wilderness', which is transformed through urbanization
processes such as flight routes, shipping lanes, finance, wi-fi networks,
policies and planning regimes.[32]

The 'city' has not disappeared, but its importance is recast as but one
moment in broader urban changes, rather than the only moment. The
transformation of the urban fabric through extended urbanization processes – mass rural population displacement, deforestation in the
Amazon, the internet – is instead elevated. Their aim is to profoundly
unsettle current understandings around what constitutes the urban and
how this might be redefined within the context of global climate change.

Nothing, they argue, lies outside the urban within a planetary
urbanization framework – 'the urban without an outside'[33] encompasses the whole world – and increasingly the spaces beyond our
worlds, with the very real prospect of interplanetary urbanization
through space exploration, travel, and tourism.

Not all agree. The thesis of 'the urban is everything' has been critiqued by those who seek to give critical voice to cultural difference
and spatial agency. Berkeley planning professor Ananya Roy highlights that the rural is not simply an antonym to the urban, but a
necessary supplement serving different socio-spatial conditions. For
example, in her essay 'What is urban about critical urban theory?' she
argues that the process of becoming urban is always incomplete, and
that 'the urban question' is intimately entangled with – not separate to
– 'the rural question'.

> I want to argue that the rural is much more than the nonurban ...
> This means that even if we are to concede the urbanization of
> everything, everywhere, we have to analytically and empirically
> explain the processes through which the urban is made, lived, and
> contested – as a circuit of capital accumulation, as a governmental
> category, as a historical conjuncture.[34]

A special issue of the journal *Society and Space*, focused on
'Placing planetary urbanization in other fields of vision', highlights
the significance of ordinary cities and citizens and the danger of
erasure of marginalized communities and voices on the global periphery through an extension of the colonial gaze. The persistence of
the city as an important site of everyday political struggle is strongly
reinforced.[35]

In response, Brenner and Schmidt argue planetary urbanization is
not 'an urbanization-as-homogenization argument or a simple spreading of a single form, across the territory or the world'. Instead 'it's an
unevenly woven, constantly imploding and exploding, fabric of social
relations, struggles, experiences, strategies'.[36]

Urbanization and its links to capitalism is one of the key challenges
underpinning the crisis of global climate change. Adjusting the frame
of how and by what means we seek to understand cities and urban life
is a contemporary paradigm shift that opens up challenges, but also
opportunities. To this, British geographer Andy Merrifield poses the
question, 'How shall we reclaim the shapeless, formless and bound-
less metropolis as a theoretical object and political object of the progressive struggle, and what, exactly, are urban politics?'[37]

And what does this mean for 21st century *urban* planning?

Planning in Pandora's shadow

For many people, the world is exploding – population, carbon,
capitalism, climate-induced disasters – as it labours under the weight
of urbanization processes and climate change. Fifty years ago, Jewish-
German philosopher Hannah Arendt published *The Human Condition*. The human *condition* she asserted, is not the same as human
nature. Written in part as a response to the development of the
atomic bomb, she refers to a quote by American physicist Robert
Oppenheimer:

> You see something that is technically sweet and you go ahead and
> do it and you argue about what to do about it only after you have

had your technical success. This is the way it was with the atomic bomb.[38]

Arendt offers two images of human activity. The first is *Animal laborans* – the beasts of burden absorbed in tasks that shut out the world. In the act of making, nothing else matters and the work becomes an end to itself. The second is *Homo faber*, who is focused on thinking and making a life in common. We can toil making things, or we can ask about the nature of the ends we pursue. Whilst *Animal laborans* is fixated on the question of 'how' things work, *Homo faber* asks 'why'.

Her thesis is that history has shown our capacity to make things, often very well – is not enough. We can build cities for example, but in their current form they are contributing to global warming and will not sustain the population. For Arendt, we need to temper the desire to 'do' with pausing to consider why and for what ends. Arendt's faith was in public speech and action, politics, and critical reflection – that it would be the capacity to think, and the powers of judgement, that will save humanity from itself. 'A life without speech and action is literally dead to the world.'[39] She affirms the possibility of thoughtful action as a critical and necessary response to dark times.

Urban social theorist Richard Sennett takes a different tack. A former student of Arendt, Sennett specifically addresses this through the idea of *craft* – not as mindless technique or procedure, but as an intimate connection between head and hand. An urban planner in a past life, Sennett seeks to restore respect for the role of *Animal laborans* by asserting that rather than a divide with *Homo faber*, the two are able to be bridged through the development of skill, commitment, and judgement. He argues that a divide between 'doing' and 'thinking' as separate activities is an artifice.

The craftsman must ask 'why' as well as 'how' about any project, including planning cities and urban regions. In this way he argues 'the craftsman can stand in Pandora's shadow – but then step out of it'.

> To understand Homo faber's role in the city we have to conceive of the dignity of labour differently. Rather than espousing a world-view, Homo faber in the city acquires honour by practicing in a way whose terms are modest ... This ethic of making modestly implies in turn a certain relationship with the city ... the physical environment seems to emanate from how we dwell and who we are.[40]

In the art of craftsmanship, thinking and feeling, action and reflection, problem solving and problem finding form a co-constituted rhythm, not separated. Sennett stresses, however, that there is nothing inevitably ethical about craft building. The craftsman's desire for quality, for example, can pose a danger. Obsession with the task can deform the work itself and the work can be morally ambiguous. Oppenheimer, for example, was a committed craftsman who pushed his technical skills to the limit to make the best bomb he could. There are numerous examples of urban planning that are technically sound but have resulted in alienating, inequitable, dispiriting, soul-destroying, and even inhumane built environments.

> ... cities as shadowlands: anonymous, homogenous and lacking character and identity; endless sprawl; polluted, unhealthy, tiring, overwhelming, confusing, alienating; cities with little connectivity or potency as *demos* – the populace of a democracy as a political unit.[41]

Urban planning has been described as the 'governance of shared places' or 'imagining the many on the move' as urban planning doyenne Patsy Healey describes.[42] This involves – but is not limited to – the circulation of people, activities, capital, non-human species, materials, and resources as part of the creativity and complexity of urban life.

The key problem arises when there is a disconnect between the values of those tasked with 'building' and those of the citizens or polity. This creates a critical tension for those who seek to enrich citizen experience and environments. Given the hybridity, entanglement, and flow of urban life, for geographer Jean Hillier, planning can only ever be experimental or speculative.

Our cities are expressions of urban life that are simultaneously both place and process; a physical, functional entity; and a particular type of cultural and social mentality. *Cité* in French refers both to a geographical place and attachment to the character of place – a kind of consciousness. At one level, this is about the 'transient, fleeting, contingent' nature of urban life, but at another there is a deeply felt commitment to building the city-state or polis and dwelling in local neighbourhoods and communities. For Sennett, this is about active citizenship – an urban politics of dwelling that seeks to find expression in how cities are built.[43]

This is at the heart of the planner's dilemma. There is too often a misfit between the 'lived experience' of the urban, and the 'building' of the city. Should urban planners seek to represent society, or try to change it? How do you translate justice into physical form? Whose justice is being served by both urban planners and social movements?[44] This involves navigating relationships that are continually being recast by changing actors and situations within the context of the contemporary city in a climate of change – carbon loaded, fluid and unbound.[45]

Beyond borders

The twenty-first-century city looms large as an omnipotent – all powerful and all seeing – construct of intersecting urban worlds. There are no limits it seems to the prospects and possibilities of the contemporary city, from geopolitical global pressure-points, to national engines and symbols, to localized culture, to imagined communities. Increasingly porous and pervasive – often aggressive and invasive – in both nature and context, they can be celebrated, suffered or resisted, but they cannot be ignored.

Cities and their citizens are not hermetically sealed, isolated, and airtight. They are increasingly fluid and agile. Yet they are strangely impotent and immobilized in the face of impending and catastrophic climate change. What is going on?

Within urban contexts, the construction of borders has helped shape and define how space, place, and experience are understood and planned for. Borders work to divide – be it landscapes, communities or ideas – and legitimize particular types of ideology, activities, or approaches. This can take on many different forms, including the physical dimensions of place, geo-administrative functions and political-economic structures of territory, sociocultural imaginings of community and globalized flows of space.

Just as maps are now understood as potent reflectors of geopolitics, real or imagined borderlines hold power and meaning, which manifests through material resources and institutional practices. They are as much about value claims on knowledge, space, and place, as any lived, cartographic, or regulatory reality no matter how problematic they have become – for example, us vs. them, friend vs. enemy, right vs. wrong, human vs. non-human, living vs. non-living.

The nature and effect of borders both shape and define the urban realm: *psychologically* through the legacy of past events and experiences uncovering prejudices, clichés, and anxieties rooted in the absence and/or failure of communities to articulate a common memory; *culturally* via a history of protracted differences, inequalities and injustices in power, policymaking, regulation and investment; and *politically* as a result of conceptual, administrative, and physical divisions reinforced by the impression of the border as a dividing line, creating difficulties in bridging the 'bordering gap'.[46]

Borders become elements of control as they shape and define how particular issues, spaces, and places are understood and acted upon such as the urban/non-urban, human/non-human, and public/private, as emotional landscapes of control. They 'exist on and through various spatial scales and are related to a number of social practices and discourses in which they are produced and made meaningful'.[47] This is then felt by communities on a wide scale, exploited through the governance of public and private space, critical infrastructure, and ecosystem services. Borders such as 'us versus them', 'friend versus enemy', or 'safety versus risk' are painfully and at times brutally reinforced as the global plight of refugees has demonstrated.

But borders are best understood not as 'the final frontiers but rather zones of interpenetration'.[48] If exposed, they can be challenged and changed. Nature in cities has traditionally been considered 'not pure enough to be true areas of ecological significance and not human enough to be politically significant'.[49] Disrupting the notion that cities are only about people helps to break down the divisions between humans and non-humans, which can lead to alternate futures.

The human condition has now become the urban condition and also the earth's condition. The convergence of urbanization and climate change calls for a reimagining of existing borders around the urban sphere vis-à-vis biosphere. The division of human and non-human, underpinned by a concept of 'civilization', is premised on the exclusion of the 'uncivilized' non-human. Can humans sustain a vision of themselves in their habitats that embraces the wild? Coming to grips with 'wild cities' is part of a wider project of dismantling human exceptionalism, but also better recognizing our own invested role. As Arendt explicitly states:

> The earth is the very quintessence of the human condition, and earthly nature, for all we know, may be unique in the universe for providing human beings with a habitat in which they can move and breathe without effort and without artifice. The human artifice of the world separates human existence from all mere animal environment, but life itself is outside this artificial world, and through life [we] remain related to all other living organisms.[50]

In finding *Homo urbanis* we are coming home – to ourselves. The problem is, we may not like very much what we see when we get there. Fixated like Klee's *Angelus Novella*, we stare open-eyed and with hands in the air at the urban storm descending upon us. Like Nemo and his friends having escaped from the city back to the sea but still floating helplessly in the harbour trapped in a sealed plastic bag, we call out, 'now what?'

Fluidity, as described by sociologist Zygmunt Bauman, is the opposite to that which is solid, permanent, and whole and cannot easily hold its shape. As Bauman observes, 'The extraordinary mobility of fluids is what associates them with the idea of lightness.' They travel easily and 'flow', 'spill', 'run out', 'splash', 'pour over', 'leak', 'flood', 'spray', 'drip', 'seep', and 'ooze', and serve as a useful metaphor for the urban in late modernity.[51] Fluidity, like carbon, defies borders, and points to the paradoxical situation we find ourselves in our cities.

We still have the capacity to take individual and collective action in the face of the coming storm. The question is, will we? And will we act in time? Can we learn to learn – and listen? Back in Melbourne, the last word goes to Australian Indigenous writer Tony Birch reflecting on the Melbourne urban context..

> The building of the Eastern Freeway required the obliteration of a vital section of the river at its confluence with the Merri Creek, a once majestic waterway winding its way into the north across Wurundjeri land. The Merri ... faces a daily battle against urbanisation in the form of household rubbish, chemical waste and weed infestation. If our river and creek valleys are 'the lungs of the city', historically we have forced them to breathe toxins.[52]

Notes

1 Barret, M (2016) 'City in the Sky', ABC documentary, accessed on https://iview.abc.net.au/show/city-in-the-sky

2 Tabuchi, H (2019) 'Worse than Anyone Expected – Air Travel Emissions Vastly Outpace Expectations', *The New York Times*, 20 September, accessed on www.nytimes.com/2019/09/19/climate/air-travel-emissions.html

3 Art Gallery of New South Wales, Brett Whiteley Studio, Surrey, accessed on https://m.artgallery.nsw.gov.au/collection/works/1.1977/

4 UN (2016) The Urban Agenda, accessed on http://habitat3.org/the-new-urban-agenda/

5 Davison, A and Mulligan, M (2004) Dissolving the Boundaries of the City: Eco-imagination and the Ecology of Compassionate Democracy, in Willis, E and Camden, P (eds) *Lifelong Learning and the Democratic Imagination*, Post Pressed, Eumundi, Chapter 4, pp. 75–99.

6 Porter, L (2018) 'From an Urban Country to Urban *Country*: Confronting the Cult of Denial in Australian Cities', *Australian Geographer*, 49(2): 239–46.
7 Ibid., p. 239.
8 Currie J (2008) 'Bo-ra-ne Ya-goo-na Par-ry-boo-go Yesterday Today Tomorrow: An Aboriginal History of Willoughby', Willoughby City Council, accessed on www.willoughby.nsw.gov.au/library/history-at-willoughby/publications/bo-ra-ne-ya-goo-na-par-ry-boo-go/
9 Clark, L (2015) 'One-tenth of Native Animals in Australia Are Extinct', *Smithsonian Magazine*, 11 February, accessed on www.smithsonianmag.com/smart-news/why-one-tenth-australias-native-mammals-have-gone-extinct-over-last-200-years-180954216/
10 Woinarski, J, Burbidge, A, Harrison, P (2015) 'Ongoing Unravelling of a Continental Fauna: Decline and Extinction of Australian Mammals Since European Settlement', in Bond, W (ed.), *Proceedings of the National Academy of Science of the United States of America*, April, accessed on www.pnas.org/content/112/15/4531?sid=3fe3987e-73d0-442a-9f32-723f17c47f70
11 Blainey, G (2001) *The Tyranny of Distance*, Macmillan Australia, Sydney.
12 Cannon, M (1975) *Life in the Cities: Australia in the Victorian Age: 3*, Thomas Nelson Ltd, Edinburgh, pp. 10–11.
13 Horne, D (1980) *A Time of Hope*, Angus and Robertson, London.
14 Birch, T (2018) 'Recovering a Narrative of Place: Stories in the Time of Climate Change', in Schultz, J (ed.), *First Things First, Griffith Review* 60, Brisbane.
15 Troy, P (ed.) (1995) *Australian Cities: Issues, Strategies and Policies for Urban Australia in the 1990s*, Cambridge University Press, Cambridge, p. ix.
16 Kelly, JF and Donegan, P (2015) *City Limits – Why Australia's Cities are Broken and How We Can Fix Them*, Melbourne University Publishing, Melbourne.
17 Richardson, S (2018) Australia has the wealth to ensure a sustainable future but too many people are being left behind, in 'The Conversation', 24th September, accessed on https://theconversation.com/australia-has-the-wealth-to-ensure-a-sustainable-future-but-too-many-people-are-being-left-behind-102979
18 Feagin, J (ed.) (1973) *The Urban Scene; Myths and Realities*, Random House, Toronto, pp. 1–2.
19 Benjamin, W (1969) *Illuminations*, Schocken, New York pp. 257–8.
20 'Angelus Novus' at the Israel Museum, Jerusalem, accessed on www.imj.org.il/en/collections/199799?itemNum=199799
21 Benjamin, W cited in Eagleton, T (2009) 'Waking the Dead', *New Statesman America*, 12 November, accessed on www.newstatesman.com/ideas/2009/11/past-benjamin-future-obama
22 Solnit, R (2016) *Hope in the Dark: Untold Histories, Wild Possibilities*, Canongate Books, New York, pp. 70–2.
23 Australian Museum, accessed on https://australianmuseum.net.au/learn/science/human-evolution/homo-sapiens-modern-humans/
24 Steele, W, Davison, A, and Reed, A (2020) 'Imagining Dirty Green Cities', in *Australian Geographer*, available online at www.tandfonline.com/doi/abs/10.1080/00049182.2020.1727127?journalCode=cage20
25 Porter, L and Yiftachel, O (2017) 'Urbanizing Settler-colonial Studies' Introduction to the Special Issue, Settler-colonial Studies, 9(2): 177.

26 Sudjic, D (2017) *The Language of Cities*, Penguin, London.
27 Ibid.
28 Mumford, L (1961) *The City in History*, Harcourt Publishing, New York, p. 53.
29 Ibid.
30 Lefebvre, H (2003) (originally 1970) *The Urban Revolution*, University of Minnesota Press, Minnesota.
31 Merrifield, A 'The Urban Question Under Planetary Urbanization', *International Journal of Urban and Regional Research*, 37(3): 909–22.
32 Brenner N and Schmid C (2015) 'Towards a New Epistemology of the Urban?' *City* 19(29): 151–82.
33 Ibid.
34 Roy A (2016) 'What is Urban about Critical Urban Theory?' *Urban Geography*, 37(6): 810–23.
35 Peake, L (2018) 'Placing Planetary Urbanization in Other Fields of Vision', *Environment and Planning D: Society and Space*, 36(3): 374–86.
36 Brenner N (2018) Debating Planetary Urbanization: For an Engaged Pluralism, Environment and Planning D', *Society and Space*, 36(3): 570–90.
37 Merrifield, A 'The Urban Question under Planetary Urbanization', *International Journal of Urban and Regional Research*, 37(3): 909–22.
38 Arendt, H (1958) *The Human Condition*, Chicago University Press, Chicago.
39 Ibid., p. 2.
40 Sennett, R (2008) *The Craftsman*, Yale University Press, London.
41 Amin, A (2006) 'The Good City', *Urban Studies*, 43(5–6): 1009–23.
42 Healey, O (2006) *Urban Complexity and Spatial Strategies – Towards a Relational Planning of Our Times*, Routledge, London.
43 Sennett, R (2018) *Ethics for the City*, Penguin, Milton Keynes, p. 1.
44 Ibid., pp. 3–4.
45 Ibid., p. 26.
46 Adapted from Herrschel, T (2011) *Borders in Post-Socialist Europe*, Ashgate, Farnham.
47 Paasi, A (2011) 'A Border Theory: An Unattainable Dream or a Realistic Aim for Border Scholars?'. In Wasti-Walter, D (ed.), *The Ashgate Companion to Border Studies*, Ashgate, Farnham, pp. 11–33.
48 Delanty, G and Rumford, C (2005) *Re-Thinking Europe: Social Theory and the Implications of Europeanization*, Routledge, London.
49 Hinchliffe, S, Kearnes, MB, Degen, M, and Whatmore, S (2005) 'Urban Wild Things: A Cosmopolitical Experiment', *Environment and Planning D: Society and Space*, 23(5): 643–58.
50 Arendt, H (1958) *The Human Condition*, Chicago University Press, Chicago, p. 2.
51 Bauman, Z (2000) *Liquid Modernity*, Polity, Cambridge.
52 Birch, T (2018) 'Recovering a Narrative of Place: Stories in the Time of Climate Change', in Schultz, J (ed.), *First Things First, Griffith Review*, 60, Brisbane.

The Living Dead (Photographer: Jesse Hales)

3   Through the security glass darkly

We be monsters

What is it about monsters we are drawn to?

In Joseph Conrad's *Heart of Darkness*, the main Western character – the trading commander Kurtz – lies dying in the Congo jungle, and barely conscious cries out, 'The horror! The horror!' His descent into darkness symbolizes the capacity for individuals, and humankind more broadly, to create catastrophic conditions of their own making. This is at one level the fabled story of the European 'gone native' and reinforcement of the perils of the wild 'other'.

> 'The wilderness' had possessed Kurtz, 'loved him, embraced him, got into his veins' – it is no wonder that Marlow [another key character] feels creepy all over just thinking about it.[1]

More deeply, it reflects the brutality, madness, evil deeds, and exploitative actions that highlight the worst aspects of Western imperialism and colonization, the deep-set contradictions of the civilizing impulse and indeed, the contradictions of the human soul. The insanity evident in the dying figure of Kurtz symbolizes just how profoundly he has lost his way. In this moment just before death he seems perhaps to grasp the extent of the monster he has become, the depth of the corruption and evil in his own heart, reflected in the values and conditions that surround him: the horror of the darkness at home and abroad – a living hell.

Film critic Noel Carrol points to the paradox in our attraction to horror books and films. Why are we often attracted to monsters? How can we find pleasure in what by nature should typically repel us? His argument is that horror is compelling because it generates experiences of fear, revulsion, distress, and disgust, which are usually avoided in everyday life. Horror juxtaposes normality with monsters. We are drawn to the idea that 'monsters do exist' and that we may be able to overcome them. Increasingly, we understand we might even be them. Monsters are both unknown and unknowable. Monsters can reveal 'the origin, identity, purposes and powers' of the monster, and in doing so, ourselves.[2] As anthropologist Hariz Halilovich notes, drawing on his own experience with those who have experienced forced displacement and diaspora in Bosnia, what is really frightening is that monstrosity is real.[3] To this end we need to 'acknowledge and remember our potent monsters now more than ever, to tell us where and who we really are, which can help us navigate our current, deep malaise'.

So often the monster is not so impossible to imagine: not science-fiction, or fantasy, or an unknown. A global pandemic like *coronavirus*, for example, a bushfire, drought, or flood, or a global corporation or system can take on a monstrous life of its own, full of unimaginable horror. Conjuring up monsters sheds light on 'the many human follies and tragedies caused by overconfidence', and an anthropocentric anxiety about speciesism, in particular 'the porousness of boundaries between different species'. The irony is that it is the human who is the one species that does not fit in, 'the freak of nature who has no place in the natural order and is capable of re-combining nature's products into hideous new forms'.[4]

The monster metaphor has been used to describe multinational corporations and more broadly the growth of capitalism and economic ideologies which underpins them, from the fearsome Scandinavian sea monster 'The Kraken', to the blood-sucking vampire, to Frankenstein and the zombie walking, the living un-dead.[5]

Perhaps these 'monsters' embody the fear that already exists – or is yet to come – as the human psyche continually throws up new configurations of the monster. The 'Corporate Frankenstein Monster' is a descriptor of 'plundering, pillaging, and polluting the planet for profit'.[6] Corporations operate as legal entities entitled to most of the rights and responsibilities that individuals possess. They can enter contracts, lend and borrow money, sue and be sued, hire employees, and own assets.

A corporation is separate and distinct from its owners, which minimizes the risk for stakeholders and investors. It operates as if a living person can – and often does – aggressively assert their legal rights in relation to economic (self)-interest. Over the past few decades, corporate rights have expanded and the process of incorporation has been simplified, yet the impacts on both the global environment and precarity of culture and society are significant – some say monstrous.

Given what these big corporations routinely do we have to ask: are they filled and peopled from top to bottom by ruthless monsters who care nothing about others, and also nothing about the world we live in? Are these CEOs and managers and stockholders so beyond human that the deaths in Iraq and Afghanistan and the destitution of the farmers and the tumours and allergies of children, and the melting of the Greenland ice cap and the shifting of the Gulf Stream are, to them, just the cost of doing business? Or are they just beyond stupid and blind, so that they, alone among humans, have no understanding of the interconnectedness of all natural systems?[7]

For Marx, these monsters of capitalism were like predatory vampires, circulating things which gain energy only by preying upon 'living labour'.[8] The fixation with the zombie apocalypse takes a different tack with its focus on a post-human world of mindless, soulless consumers. This is 'part of the realization that the logical evolution of global capitalism leads to nothing but destruction and tied to the conviction that there is no possible alternative to capitalism as a worldwide economic system'.[9]

If the modern vampire may have functioned as an apt metaphor for the predatory practices of capital in colonial and post-colonial societies, today's zombie hordes may best express our anxieties about capitalism's apparently inevitable by-products: the legions of mindless, soulless consumers who sustain its endless production, and the masses of 'human debris' who are left to survive the ravages of its poisoned waste.[10]

'A Zombie Manifesto: The Nonhuman Condition in the Era of Advanced Capitalism' proposed by Sarah Juliet Lauro and Karen Embry also envisages the zombie as modern-day consumer, one that is 'trapped within the ideological construct that assures the survival of the system. The zombie illustrates humanity's attempt to transfer its burden onto others – as well as our fears of increasingly publicized diseases. In its frenzied state of pure consumption, the zombie seeks to infect those who do not yet share in the oppression of their state'.[11]

Climate denial, carbon emissions, and *coronavirus* writ large.

In a bizarre self-parodying moment, cities across the world hold annual Zombie Walks. In zombie costumes, citizens march the city streets rallying for 'zombie rights'. The Zombie Walk in Minneapolis–Saint Paul in the United States, for example, attracted 8,027 participants, whilst approximately 15,000 people took to the streets of Santiago in Chile to take part in the city's fourth annual Zombie Walk.[12] In Melbourne, the un-dead converge for the annual Zombie Shuffle with 'hordes of zombies expected to stagger, groan and grunt their way' through the city.[13]

Researchers have investigated whether humanity can survive a zombie outbreak, and if so how. A Zombie Apocalypse Index (ZAI) was developed at Cornell University to assess which American cities were best equipped to deal with the 'un-dead'. Cities were ranked according to the quality and capacity for defence, containment, cure research, and food supply.[14] One of the defining features to surviving the zombie apocalypse is population proximity – the higher the population proximity, the greater the threat. We are seeing this now with the coronavirus.

The key message of zombie culture – live as far away from the major cities as possible. The best chance for survival, according to the ZAI, is to be located in remote or sparsely populated or proximate areas.

> 'It's bad to be near any big city. Just look at the population map. First, you'd benefit from the fact that it would be highly unlikely for the zombie outbreak to begin where you are, and then it would take a very long time for any zombies to get out there.'[15]

In Australia, a Zombie Survival Index (ZSI) ranking has been developed by researchers from the Centre for Disaster Management and Public Safety at the University of Melbourne. The ZSI models major cities across Australia and New Zealand based on criteria related to how well they would handle a life-altering outbreak. Different criteria included the potential rate of zombie infection; situational analysis of the infection's origin; how the disease would spread; how residents claim they would act; and how well each city would defend itself against the walking dead and geographical location. As professor Greg Foliente, the centre's deputy director warns, in all cities, this involves a fight and flight tactical strategy.

> You need to build a defensive ring around the source of any attack to overpower the zombies with numbers, because if you

miss that chance, they will just overpower everyone as long as they have contact with a population. Alternatively, if you have enough warning, disperse as fast as you can.[16]

Radical philosopher Slavoj Žižek observes 'it's much easier to imagine the end of all life on Earth than a much more modest radical change in capitalism'.[17] Alternatively, 'we can now revise that and witness the attempt to imagine capitalism by way of imagining the end of the world' according to philosopher Fredric Jameson in an article entitled 'Future City'.[18]

The city of extremes

The city is us and we are it, a mirror to the sinner and saint, the maverick and monster within. As monsters, the 'regions of human practice where old or established boundaries are being challenged by new ensembles and configurations'.[19] Such monsters can disrupt rigid hierarchies by 'throwing conventional polarities into disorder – mind/body, human/animal, alive/dead, natural/unnatural, tame/wild, self/other, same/different, inside/outside, imaginary/real, conception/perception, human/non-human, us/them, living/dead etc.'[20]

Ashley Dawson coined the term 'extreme cities' and is the author of *Extinction: A Radical History*. The 'extreme' moniker refers to the global convergence of climate change and urbanization amidst conditions of economic divide, species extinction, and unsustainable development; an urban fabric of stark inequality slung between the two opposing poles of the contemporary urban imaginary, 'a paradigm of technological sophistication and orderliness, and the other a sprawl of decaying infrastructure and informal settlements'.[21]

The city, Dawson argues, is where capitalism's central contradictions play havoc, with no quick *quid pro quo*, or quick city fix.

We certainly need technology and planning to help adapt to the climate chaos, but under present social conditions, these tools are more likely to be employed by elites to create architectures of apartheid and exclusionary zones of refuge.[22]

Four key urban contradictions and paradoxes around which the city is contested are outlined by urban planning professor Robert Beauregard: wealth and poverty, destruction and sustainability, oligarchy and democracy, and intolerance and tolerance.[23] These contradictions are not seen as polar opposites but instead two sides of the

same urban coin. As one might positively describe a lover's characteristics in the throes of an affair or relationship – passion, commitment,
energy, care – these very same characteristics can be seen to be negative once the affair is ended – obsession, control, hyperactivity, nar-
cissism. And so it is with our cities.

Cities generate the largest environmental destruction on the planet
and yet also offer opportunities for achieving environmental sustainability and a low-carbon future. The sheer scale of cities magnifies
their capacity for destruction, exacerbated by unsustainable patterns
of production and consumption. Energy usage, home and car ownership, pollution, waste, and the sprawl of impervious surfaces that have
buried rivers and gobbled up rural hinterlands, have an ongoing and
devastating impact.

The extensive ecological footprint of cities extends far past the
regulatory borders, far exceeding the carrying capacity of the land
they inhabit. For the majority of the population of the Global North,
'living locally' means almost total reliance on carbon-intensive indus-
tries, systems, and transport infrastructures from afar for food, water,
and energy. The key to sustainability is a low-carbon future that recal-
ibrates carbon- and energy-intensive life-support systems for cities.

The second paradox is the extent to which cities have the ability to
generate and concentrate both great wealth and great poverty. Some
people are disproportionately wealthy (i.e. the few), while for others
poverty has become so thoroughly entrenched (i.e. the many). Private
wealth depends on the public wealth and investment in infrastructure
and institutional apparatus, yet the distribution of the benefits for all
citizens has become skewed towards the elite and privileged in contemporary capitalist utopias 'where consumption and inequality
surpass our worst nightmares threatened by savage capitalism that
seems poised to consume all of the Earth's resources in a single
generation'.[24]

This is fuelled by the third paradox which is the capacity of cities
to promote democracy and at the same time create the conditions for
political oppression and exploitation. A politics of co-existence and
encounter through living in close proximity has led to the belief that
the story of [Western] cities, is the story of democracy. However, this
must be balanced against the concentrated power and privilege that
works against participation and silences political dissent.

In countries like Australia, the establishment of the major cities
through the twin processes of invasion and genocide is synonymous
with 'development' and 'progress'. This manifests through the twin
processes of urbanization and a racist imaginary that locates cities in

settler-colonial societies on unceded Indigenous land: one that first colonizes Indigenous land for urban development and then proceeds to render Indigenous owners as invisible. The colonial-settler city is both insidious and disingenuous,

> … often portrayed as a symbol of a 'new world', a space of liberalism and democracy, a hub of globalization, a magnet for international migration, or a center of investment and corporate power – all dominant discourses that conceal their ongoing colonial nature. Such cities are symbols of the profound displacement, erasure and often destruction of Indigenous histories and geographies and are at the same time precisely the form that keeps that displacement hidden.[25]

A fourth paradox is the way in which cities encourage and nurture tolerance, whilst simultaneously ushering in contempt, violence, discrimination and marginalization, and hate crimes. Many people are drawn to cities for the tolerance that is afforded for difference, whether it be race, sexuality, gender, ability, or age. However, intolerance through segregated spaces and unwelcoming places can be reinforced and exacerbated in cities in ways that range from the ubiquitous to blunt-edged displays of power and politics.

Organized and well-resourced special interests can shrink the public realm and capacity for real citizen engagement. The right to the city for many is not easily accessible but must be navigated and negotiated through established and entrenched power structures that can violently suppress difference. Indifference, marginalization and violence are the flipside of urban connectivity, care, and diversity.

Through the security glass darkly, the urban contradictions and architectures of fear abound. 'More than a place of extremes as if those extremes can be bridged, the city is fundamentally disordered.'[26] The dark side of the city is the poverty, slums, racial discrimination, terrorism, evil, vice, alienation, corruption, rejection. Often mean-spirited and mean-hearted, cities are both a process and a material reality, but they are the setting, not the player. The city is not the cause of the problems and paradoxes of the urban age, nor the solution. This burden and responsibility is squarely with us, the city builders and dwellers – the citizens.

For we are the monsters and 'makers' of our own fear-filled urban modernity.

Climate security

Within the major cities – where the majority of people in the world live – the immediacy and potentially catastrophic nature of climate change threaten the security of the global population, and the capacity of the planet to sustain life as we know it. The urban impacts of climate change are altering the frequency of extreme weather events such as droughts, bushfires, storm surges, cyclones, and hail. This is expected to increase damage to infrastructure, disrupt key services, increase insurance costs, and increase risk to human life including respiratory disease, heat stress, post-event disease outbreaks and other health-related impacts. The C40 Cities Climate Leadership Group advocates urgent recognition around the crucial role of cities if the 'battle' to prevent catastrophic climate change is to be 'won'.

In Australia, where the majority of the population lives in the five largest cities largely located on the vulnerable Australian coastline, climate change is an urban issue. Climate change is contributing a major threat to the health of individuals, communities, and the economy. The highly concentrated nature of urban populations, coupled with the relatively fixed nature of much of the metropolitan built form, serves to magnify climate-related risks from extreme weather and natural disasters (i.e. sea-level rise, heat waves, and drought). These include food, water, and energy scarcity; population displacement and movement; key infrastructure destruction and damage (i.e. rail, telecommunications, sewerage); and the spread of infectious diseases.

> The heatwave in Melbourne resulted in the buckling of train tracks, collapsing transport networks across the city. In addition, city morgues exceeded capacity as they managed more than twice the number of bodies than in the same period of the previous year.[27]

The speed and immediacy of climate change impacts on Australian cities and poses considerable challenges to existing institutional and governance structures. Located within Australia's three-tier federal government system, the largest cities are now recognized as having 'world city' or 'global city' status. They act as significant international nodes for economic, political, communication and cultural exchanges. Yet all Australian cities currently suffer from an absence of clear and effective metropolitan-scale arrangements for the planning of urban development, the co-ordination of urban services, and responding to climate change challenges.

A stronger national security role for Australian cities has long been advocated by urban researchers who have pointed to the disjuncture between the concentration of population and yet the absence of dedicated structures for urban decision-making for welfare and well-being at every scale, from the individual to the nation.

> The high degree of urbanisation in Australia, together with the observation that cities are major consumers of energy, water and food and emitters of greenhouse gases, means that managing our cities is an essential national issue as climate change adaptation and mitigation become increasingly important.[28]

The 2017 Senate inquiry into the implications of climate change for Australia's national security found that climate change is a direct threat to Australia's national security, which encompasses state security, human security, and the viability of infrastructure and economies.[29] The final report argued for 'a significant step-up in climate-security thinking and policy in Australia', including the development of new senior government positions; a dedicated climate-security leadership position in Home Affairs to coordinate climate resilience issues; a climate-security white paper to guide a co-ordinated government response to climate change risks; and the release by the Department of Defence of an unclassified version of the work it has undertaken already to identify climate risks in Australia.[30]

But is this too little, too slow and too late to respond to the climate change crisis? In *Requiem for a Species*, Clive Hamilton argued that governments that delay taking action on climate change will find that 'the global system will have shifted course and the future will be taken out of our hands'.[31] However, to date, addressing climate change has not generated the urgency and speed in Australia emphasized by the Intergovernmental Panel on Climate Change.

History has demonstrated that the ability to capture political imagination around matters of national risk and security tends to bring with it the institutional capacity to generate – with speed – extraordinary measures that reside outside normal democratic routines and governance processes. The Australian response to the global security climate around the 'war on terror' in the wake of the 9/11 World Trade Center tragedy exemplifies this approach. At the national level, the then Australian Minister for Foreign Affairs Alexander Downer invoked the following security rhetoric to mobilize the nation:

> We are engaged in a war to protect the very civilisation we have
> worked so hard to create – a civilisation founded on democracy,
> personal liberty, the rule of law, religious freedom and tolerance
> ... The terrorism challenge we face does have the dimensions of a
> war. Its prosecution requires: clear-sighted political commitment;
> national vigilance and preparedness; an informed and resilient
> public; and a commitment of energy and resources that must be
> sustained over many years.[32]

As a matter of national security, the Howard government fast-tracked
legislation to protect against the threat of global terrorism including new
control orders, preventative detention orders, and questioning powers.[33]
The government committed $3 billion to protecting Australia against
terrorist threats, with an additional $400 million given to Australian
intelligence, security and law-enforcement agencies to further strengthen
the nation's response, the rationale, that 'a necessary premise of any constitutional order and system of government is that people are alive ...
serious threats to national security must be addressed'.[34]

Unlike the focused and co-ordinated approach from the Australian
Government to the 'war on terror' and 'weapons of mass destruction',
national policy action around the catastrophic risks posed by climate
change – 'weather of mass destruction' – has been tentative, slow, and
deeply divided. Climate security is positioned in either the 'police
frame' (nationalistic and military association) or the 'priest frame'
(non-military, egalitarian, norms, agencies, and strategies) including a
focus on mitigation and adaptation measures through critical infrastructure and planning, strategic national defence, and growing calls
for declaring a state of climate emergency.

Climate-security narrative 1 – critical urban infrastructure

The first national climate-security narrative focuses on mitigation and
adaptation through nation-building, infrastructure, and planning. This
involves creating more resilient and equitable urban settlements
through policy and planning initiatives that address 'the very large deficits and deficiencies in basic infrastructure'.[35] Urban infrastructure
networks shape and sustain our cities as well as render them exposed
and vulnerable to a wide range of threats such as natural disasters, terrorism, peak oil and climate change. The lines drawn between what is
defined as critical and that which is not concerns not only the physical
or informational assets but also the inclusion/exclusion of communities and their places and values.

Critical infrastructure is referred to as lifelines – 'the arteries and veins of urbanized society'.[36]These are 'the basic facilities, services, and installations needed for the functioning of a community or society, such as transportation and communications systems, water and power lines, and public institutions including schools, post offices, and prisons'.[37] Infrastructure is defined as critical either explicitly or implicitly on the basis of *what is at threat* should the infrastructure be destroyed or disabled, and how much that matters. The question of 'critical how and to whom' is central.

Most critical infrastructure in Australia is privately or part-privately owned or operated. The Australian Government's *Critical Infrastructure Resilience Strategy* relies on a public–private partnership approach for national security and infrastructure provision, particularly in times of threat or disaster. In many cases there is shared ownership of, and responsibility for, infrastructure assets, and recovery from disruption is highly variable and often 'messy'.

Some infrastructure assets are solely government owned, such as some highways, dams, and catchments. Others are privately owned, such as some airports, ports, and electricity generation facilities, or owned and operated through public–private partnership arrangements, such as a toll roads and trains, electricity distribution networks, and prisons. And some infrastructure assets are community owned, such as irrigation systems and distributed energy systems. Confusion exists with respect to the ownership versus service provision arrangements for some infrastructure assets, for example, the supply and distribution of water resources from catchments.[38]

It is this variation in ownership arrangements that makes the allocation of risk and *responsibility* difficult to discern, especially for events that have yet to unfold. The *risk to* infrastructure itself and risk to communities or firms from loss or disruption on the other; and the *responsibility for* building/maintaining infrastructure and dealing with the impacts of loss or disruption on communities or firms.

This security response positions a response to climate change as subsumed under the overarching agenda vision for Australian cities that are 'productive, and globally competitive, with integrated land use, transport and infrastructure planning driving more efficient investment and outcomes'.[39] Its ambitions are for long-term city security and resilience through the funding and development of strategic plans and key urban infrastructure.

Climate-security narrative 2 – a strategic defence and military agenda

A quite different national security approach is an emphasis on strategic national defence and military agenda to be 'future-ready'. In a special report by the Australian Strategic Policy Institute, a number of recommendations are made that support the need for urgent attention to urban adaptation in light of the 'potentially devastating climate change impacts on Australian lives and property'.[40] This is envisaged to include the need for a stronger mandate (and thus funding arrangements) for security agencies such as the Australian Defence Force as a means to provide the personnel, technologies, and capabilities needed to adequately respond to climate change threats.

> Climate change works as a threat multiplier – it exacerbates the drivers of conflict by deepening fragilities within societies, straining weak institutions, reshaping power balances and undermining post-conflict recovery and peacebuilding.[41]

The *Hardening Australia* report points out that the military provide important services for urban settlements through the provision of logistic support, emergency shelter, and search for bodies in emergencies such as bushfires, floods, and drought. The argument posed is that the challenge of climate change for cities should be acknowledged as a significant national (homeland) security threat. This 'will add urgency to the issue of climate change adaptation and pose questions for long-term defence force structure decisions in areas such as remote sensing, logistics and military engineering'.[42]

An article in the *Australian Defence Magazine* entitled 'Reframing climate change as a core national security issue' argues there are at least five implicit assumptions in our security approach to climate change that are questionable and continue to fuel the political divide: Australia's policy approach is that environmental degradation and climate change are not a significant national security risk; the environment is something we can afford to consider, but only if it does not affect traditional security or economic arrangements; climate change will be slow and generational thus allowing time to prepare and respond; our systems (governance, defence, early warning, foreign policy, engineering, mitigation) are robust enough to adapt to slow-changing effects brought about by climate change; and Australians are great innovators and can always stay ahead of unwanted changes.

By contrast, a 2019 internal Australian Defence Force briefing note warned that the impacts of climate change are unavoidable and a definite threat to homeland security. 'Sea-level rise, ocean acidification, increase in extreme temperatures and a forecast increase in intensity of bushfires and extreme weather events may directly impact Defence capabilities.' Other key points include no overarching military strategy to address climate change risks, and that the Indo-Pacific region is projected to experience prolonged droughts and increased flooding from sea-level rise, which will increase the risk of conflict and climate refugees.[43]

> Today we are confronted by global environmental degradation and climate change, occurring at an unprecedented scale and speed; with cascading and ramifying risks transferred to infrastructure, energy systems and the global economy. At this scale climate change impacts at every level of our military and national security systems.[44]

Climate-security narrative 3 – declaring a state of emergency

The growing sense of urgency around the need for action on climate change has led to calls from across the community for a much swifter and more strategically co-ordinated response. There are increasingly urgent calls for 'climate change' to be reframed as a 'climate emergency' in response to the speed and scale of transition that is required.[45] This echoes the view of former United Nations Secretary General Ban Ki-Moon, who describes global warming as an emergency situation requiring emergency action.

> Imagine there is a fire in your house. What do you do? What do you think about? Your senses are heightened, you are focused like a laser, and you put your entire self into your actions. You enter emergency mode.[46]

The earth systems are in triage in response to climate change conditions that some describe as having entered the realm of a 'code red'. This will require an emergency response similar to those taken during natural disasters or wartime efforts. Environmental advocacy group The Climate Mobilization, for example, calls for people to pledge support for a World War II-scale climate mobilization – but at a scale and speed of change never seen during peacetime.

A 'code red' emergency requires 'an imaginative, large-scale programme comparable in scope to the war economy'.[47] The urgency of the climate task requires emergency measures that must disrupt the institutional status quo by invoking actions that go 'far beyond business as usual and politics as usual, to bring about a rapid transition to a post-carbon, safe-climate future'.[48]

> In emergency mode we stop 'business-as-usual' because nothing else matters as much as the crisis. We don't rush thoughtlessly in, but focus on a plan of action, which we implement with thought, and all possible care and speed, to protect others and get to safety ... A 'whatever it takes' attitude means that government plans and directs the nation's resources and capacity towards building up the war effort. This can be done at amazing speed.[49]

In inner-city Melbourne in 2016, Darebin Council became the first government in the world to declare a climate emergency, calling for urgent action by all levels of government to achieve zero emissions by 2030. This includes the following local-scale climate reform priorities: achieve 100 per cent renewable energy by 2030, then double renewable energy supply to meet all of Australia's energy needs and foster new jobs and new industry; reform planning laws and building standards to mandate that all new construction and major renovations and extensions on existing buildings deliver net zero emissions outcomes by 2023, including the removal of all requirements to connect to gas; require all products and packaging sold in Australia to be made from fully recycled material by default; require all roads and footpaths to be made with fully recycled materials; invest in the infrastructure to support the just transition to all electric cars, buses, and trucks by 2025; and support local manufacturing of all types of road transport vehicles.[50]

The City of Melbourne has also declared a climate and biodiversity emergency after councillors agreed that climate change and mass species extinction 'pose serious risks to the people of Melbourne and Australia'. The city has called upon the Australian and Victoria governments to declare a climate emergency and commit to a 1.5°C science-based target in line with the Paris Climate Agreement.

> Australia is still the largest emitter of greenhouse gas emissions per capita in the developed world. Recent data shows our emissions have increased nationally over the last four years. This is hurting our economy, our environment and our health. The recent bushfires, drought and extreme weather across Australia are evidence of this.[51]

Urban geographer Brendan Gleeson argues that Australian cities offer a set of countervailing adaptive possibilities, 'a well spring of harm, and a field of possibility; a whirlpool of failing ambition and an island of refuge and renewal'.[52] To this end, he calls for the setting up of a 'guardian state' to steer eco-cidal cities through the current climate emergency. At a practical level, the guardian state would address climate risk and security in cities through a national settlement strategy as part of an 'Australian Plan' for navigating the climate crisis. This would then be devolved to communities and local authorities to manage through metropolitan commissions.

The use of the wartime security framing and rhetoric to elevate issues has been criticized as an inappropriate basis for sustainability issues or ecologically transformative politics. The fear is that 'hanging the climate change debate on the security hook to speed up implementation' is a double-edged sword that can undermine the most basic principles of civil rights and democracy.[53] As environmental politics professor Robyn Eckersley reminds us, there are 'few green theorists who are prepared to defend the nation-state as an institution that is able to play, on balance, a positive role in securing sustainable livelihoods and ecosystem integrity'.[54]

For Gleeson, this is not envisaged as a permanent institutional transformation, but rather a 'transitional state, just as in World War II, that knows it must dissolve at the first opportunity ... rather than leaving the politics of our emergencies to the last possible moment'.[55] Consumption rights not civil rights would be circumscribed in such circumstances, underpinned by the three key ethical principles of restraint, sacrifice, and solidarity.

> We enter the storm as yet ill prepared, our urban lifeboats far from secured and provisioned for the tough journey ahead. ...The new setting, towards sustainability and security, will require a changed urban course that will take our cities through the storm ahead to more resilient shores.[56]

The age of anxiety

Our insecurity about security is underpinned by intertwined tensions of fear and hope. Fear is a primal response to either real or perceived physical and emotional danger, which can trigger fight, flight, or freeze reactions at an individual or societal scale. As Descartes observed, 'When hope is so strong that it chases out fear entirely, it changes in nature and calls itself security.'[57] One way of thinking about security is that it seeks to hold and maintain the status quo. 'Security is to keep oneself on the right side of disaster.'[58]

A different interpretation is possible, invoking the 'angel of history': 'The concept of progress must be grounded in the idea of catastrophe. That things are status quo, is the catastrophe.'[59]

> The rapid and irreversible degradation of the environment will feed ever further. As a derisory counterweight responding to each cataclysm, the myth of a society that reflects an enlightened modernity, conscious of the risks we are all running and prepared, this time, to take a measure of the dangers faced. But just as the dogma of market security considers all public intervention, we can be certain that nothing will be done to put the brakes on the untrammelled looting of the planet, blind productivism and the breakneck rise of inequalities. Security (the catastrophe) is when everything continues as before.[60]

Speaking and writing about security is never innocent and holds with it the potential to become part of the same technology that constructs and manages fear, control and order. The issue becomes one of how to engage with the security framing without just replicating dominant and exclusionary modes.[61]

Security threats are generally conceived in terms of the need for an 'enemy'. The post 9/11 call to arms by United States President George W. Bush, for example, offered a stark choice: 'Either you are with us or you are with the terrorists.'[62] The emphasis was on 'security' as a pre-existing object or fact. This was then extended to include the role of 'securitizing speech-acts'. This is the way in which specific threats are shifted from the realm of the 'normal' (i.e. the arena of democratic rules and decision-making procedures) to the 'exceptional' (characterized by the highest urgency and priority).

But securing precisely what? And for whom? When security measures are applied, it is important to understand who or what is being secured. This includes attentiveness to the casting of the security issue as an 'existential threat that necessitates the use of emergency measures; and how and in what ways this shifts beyond the everyday norms and routines'.[63] This focus on security differs from a risk management approach, which seeks to be pre-emptive through methods of risk surveillance, control, or reduction. The processes of securitization, by contrast, is a political choice and act. A sense of political community is re-established and the 'we-ness' of identity reinforced.[64]

Us (the good guys) versus them (the bad guys), this gets complicated with climate change.

Fear is a powerful emotion that shapes human actions in political,
social, economic, and environmental realms. This expansion of fear
seems to arise from many sources: threats of natural disasters, global
climate change, and health pandemics now occur alongside geopolitical fearmongering and growing apprehensions about inequality, social
injustice, and political instability.

Is there a creative space for exploration between the increasingly
human security orientation of disaster and emergency management,
and the securitization of critical infrastructure discourse? How can
natural ecosystems be better recognized and integrated as critical to
human survival and flourishing in the face of infrastructure privatiza-
tion and securitization? Where are the points of resistance and pathways for alternative action?[65]

New directions in security studies have sought to reframe security
as a positive or constructive agenda that can hold emancipatory
goals.[66] The larger geopolitical/eco-political contexts of climate change,
food, water and energy have generated a range of human security perspectives where the global nature of environmental issues that tran-
scends state boundaries and policies is highlighted. This has challenged
the focus on national security and points to the need for a more com-
prehensive understanding of security that takes 'human well-being and
ecosystem integrity, rather than states, as the fundamental moral and
analytical reference point'.[67]

A humane/environmental security approach emphasizes the protection and empowerment of those most vulnerable (both human and non-
human). This includes a rejection of the early military approach to
securitization in favour of alternative modes expressed through delibera-
tive democracy, education, and the values of compassion and caring.
The focus is on the reduction of vulnerability, community engagement,
and sharing responsibility across the community, public and private
sectors. Disasters are defined as inseparable from climate change and vulnerability and are linked closely to fear, poverty, and harm reduction.[68]

Cities are increasingly recognized as key sites of national significance
particularly vulnerable to climate change in ways that are complex and
multi-faceted. In the case of Australian cities, climate change, for
example, is expected to alter the frequency of extreme weather events
such as droughts, bushfires, storm surges, cyclones, and hail. This is
likely to increase damage to infrastructure, disrupt key services,
increase insurance costs, and increase risk to human life including respiratory disease, heat stress, post-event disease outbreaks, and other

health-related impacts. The ways in which we plan and take action in this climate of change matters.

Are we the snake or the apple? Despite the compelling nature and urgency of the climate change imperative, not all ways of presenting security threats are appropriate, and not all ways of governing in a state of emergency are equal.

We must beware the monster in the urban abyss.

Notes

1 Attridge, J (2018) 'How Conrad's Imperial Horror Story *Heart of Darkness* Resonates with our Globalised Times', 23 May, accessed on https://the-conversation.com/how-conrads-imperial-horror-story-heart-of-darkness-resonates-with-our-globalised-times-94723

2 Carrol, N (2002) 'Why Horror?', in Jancovich, N (ed.), *Horror: The Film Reader*, Routledge, New York.

3 Halovitch, H (2019) 'Vampires and Ratko Mladić: Balkan Monsters and The Monstering of People', in Lee, J, Halilovitch, H, Landau-Ward, A, Phipps, P and Sutcliffe, R (eds), *Monsters of Modernity: Global Icons for our Critical Condition*, Kismet Press, Leeds.

4 Lee, J, Halilovitch, H, Landau-Ward, A, Phipps, P and Sutcliffe, R (2019) *Monsters of Modernity: Global Icons for our Critical Condition*, Kismet Press, Leeds.

5 Pengilley, V (2018) 'From Vampires to Zombies – The Monsters We Create say a Lot About Us', ABC Radio National, 9 September, accessed on www.abc.net.au/news/2018-09-09/monsters-we-create-reflect-our-fears-and-desires/10174880

6 Finn, E (2013) 'The Corporate Frankenstein Monster', Canadian Centre for Policy Alternatives, accessed on www.policyalternatives.ca/publications/monitor/corporate-frankenstein-monster

7 Smiley, J (2005) *Good Faith*, Faber and Faber, London.

8 Castillo, D (2016) 'Zombie Masses: Monsters for the Age of Global Capitalism', in Castillo, D, Schmidt, D, Reilly, D, and Browning, J (eds), *Zombie Talk: Culture, History, Politics*, Palgrave, London, p. 43.

9 Castillo, D and Eggington, W (2014) Dreamboat Vampires and Zombie Capitalists, *The New York Times*, 26 October, accessed on https://opinionator.blogs.nytimes.com/2014/10/26/dreamboat-vampires-and-zombie-capitalists/

10 Ibid., p. 1.

11 Lauro, S and Embry, K (2008) 'A Zombie Manifesto: The Nonhuman Condition in the Era of Advanced Capitalism', *Boundary 2: An International Journal of Literature and Culture*, 35(1): 85–108.

12 'Zombie Walk', accessed on https://en.wikipedia.org/wiki/Zombie_walk

13 'Melbourne Zombie Shuffle', *Time Out*, accessed on www.timeout.com/melbourne/things-to-do/melbourne-zombie-shuffle

14 'The Zombie Apocalypse Index (ZAI)', accessed on https://public.tableau.com/profile/mary.lorenz#!/vizhome/ZombieApocalypse/FinalRankings

15 McCoy, T (2015) 'Scientists Determine the Nation's Safest Places to Ride out a Zombie Apocalypse', *The Washington Post*, 4 March, accessed on

www.washingtonpost.com/news/morning-mix/wp/2015/03/04/scientists-determine-the-nations-safest-places-to-ride-out-a-zombie-outbreak/
16 Foliente, G (2018) 'Surviving Zombie Attack', 22 May, accessed on www.unimelb.edu.au/cdmps/news/news-items/surviving-zombie-attack
17 Žižek, S (2018) *The Courage of Hopelessness: Chronicles of a Year of Living Dangerously*, Penguin, London.
18 Jameson, F (2003) 'Future City', *New Left Review*, 21, May–June.
19 Lee, J, Halilovitch, H, Landau-Ward, A, Phipps, P and Sutcliffe, R (2019) *Monsters of Modernity: Global Icons for Our Critical Condition*, Kismet Press, Leeds.
20 Ibid.
21 Dawson, A (2017) *Extreme Cities: The Peril and Promise of Urban Life in the Age of Climate Change*, Verso, London, p. 6.
22 Ibid., p. 9.
23 Beauregard, R (2018) *Cities in the Urban Age: A Dissent*, The University of Chicago Press, Chicago.
24 Davis, M and Monk, D (eds) (2007) *Evil Paradises: Dreamworlds of neo-liberalism*, The New Press, New York.
25 Porter, L and Yiftachel, O (2017) Urbanizing Settler-colonial Studies: Introduction to the Special Issue, *Settler-colonial Studies*, 9(2): 177–86.
26 Beauregard, R (2018) *Cities in the Urban Age: A Dissent*, University of Chicago Press, Chicago.
27 Australian Government. (2010) *State of Australian Cities Report 2010*, Major Cities Unit Sydney: Infrastructure Australia, p. 94.
28 ATSE. (2010) *Climate Change and the Urban Environment: Managing Our Urban Areas in a Changing Environment*, Workshop Report, Carlton, Melbourne Business School.
29 Parliament of Australia (2017) *Senate Inquiry Into the Implications of Climate Change for Australia's National Security*, accessed on www.aph.gov.au/Parliamentary_Business/Committees/Senate/Foreign_Affairs_Defence_and_Trade/Nationalsecurity
30 Macdonald, M (2020) 'Climate Change, Security and the Australian Bushfires, Lowry Institute', 12 February, accessed on www.lowyinstitute.org/the-interpreter/climate-change-security-and-australian-bushfires
31 Hamilton, C (2010) *Requiem for a Species – Why We Resist the Truth About Climate Change*, Allen & Unwin, Crows Nest, p. 225.
32 Downer, A. (2004) 'Australia and the Threat of Global Terrorism – A Test of Resolve', Speech to the National Press Club, Canberra, 13 April.
33 Ruddock, P. (2007) 'Law as a Preventative Weapon Against Terrorism', in Lynch, A, MacDonald, E, and Williams, G (eds), *Law and Liberty in the War on Terror*, The Federation Press, Sydney.
34 Ibid., p. 3.
35 Satterthwaite, D, Huq, S, Reid, H, Pelling, M, and Lankao, P. (2009) 'Adapting to Climate Change in Urban Areas: The Possibilities and Constraints in Low- and Middle-Income Nations', in Bicknell, J, Dodman, D, and Satterthwaite, D (eds), *Adapting Cities to Climate Change: Understanding and Addressing the Development Challenges*, London, Earthscan, London, pp. 3–34.
36 De Bruijne, M and Van Eaten, M (2007) 'Systems that Should Have Failed: Critical Infrastructure Protection in an Institutionally Fragmented Environment', *Journal of Contingencies and Crisis Management* 15(1): 18–29.

37 Moteff, J and Paul, P (2004) 'Critical Infrastructure and Key Assets: Definition and Identification'. CRS Report for Congress, CR Service, The Library of Congess, Washington, DC, p. 17.
38 Hussey, K and Dovers, S (2015) 'Managing Critical Infrastructure in a Changing Climate: Risk, Roles, Responsibilities and Politics', *Proceedings of the Research Forum, Bushfire and Natural Hazards, and AFAC Conference*, Wellington NZ, 2 September 2014.
39 Australian Government. (2010) 'State of Australian Cities Report 2010', Major Cities Unit, Infrastructure Australia, Sydney, p. 1.
40 Yates, A and Bergin, A (2009) 'Hardening Australia: Climate Change and Natural Disaster Resilience', Australian Strategic Policy Institute, Issue 24, August, p. 1.
41 Barrie, C (2019) 'Climate Change Poses a Direct Threat to Australia's National Security', *The Strategist, Australian Strategic Policy*, 9 October, accessed on www.aspistrategist.org.au/climate-change-poses-a-direct-threat-to-australias-national-security/
42 Yates, A and Bergin, A (2009) 'Hardening Australia: Climate Change and Natural Disaster Resilience', Australian Strategic Policy Institute, 24, August, p. 3.
43 Willacy, M (2019) 'Defence Lacks "Overarching Strategy" to Deal with Climate Change Conflict', ABC News, 15 July, accessed on www.abc.net.au/news/2019-07-15/defence-lacks-overarching-strategy-for-climate-change-conflict/11304954
44 Institute for Integrated Economics Research (IIER) (2019) 'Reframing Climate Change as a Core National Security Issue', *Australian Defence Magazine*, 6 June, accessed on www.australiandefence.com.au/defence/budget-policy/reframing-climate-change-as-a-core-national-security-issue
45 Spratt, D and Sutton, P (2007) *Climate Code Red*, Scribe Publications, Melbourne.
46 Klein Salamon, M. (2016) 'Leading the Public into Emergency Mode: A New Strategy for the Climate Movement', accessed on https:// www.theclimatemobilization.org/emergency-mode
47 Spratt, D and Sutton, P (2007) *Climate Code Red*, Scribe Publications, Melbourne, p. 1.
48 Ibid.
49 Gilding, P (2019) 'Climate Emergency Defined', Breakthrough – National Centre for Climate Restoration Melbourne, accessed on https://52a87f3e-7945-4bb1-abbf-9aa66cd4e93e.filesusr.com/ugd/148cb0_3be3bfab3f3a489c b9bd69e42ce22e7c.pdf
50 Darebin Council, Climate Emergency.
51 City of Melbourne to commit to a 1.5°C science-based target in line with the Paris Climate Agreement.
52 Gleeson, BJ (2010) *Lifeboat Cities*, University of New South Wales Press, Sydney, p. 104.
53 Brown, O. (2007) 'Weather of Mass Destruction? The Rise of Climate Change as The "New" Security Issue'. Commentary, International Institute for Sustainable Development, December, p. 2.
54 Eckersley, R. (2005) 'Greening the Nation-state: From Exclusive to Inclusive Sovereignty', in Barry, J and Eckersley, R (eds), *The State and the Global Ecological Crisis*, Massachusetts Institute of Technology, Cambridge, MA, p. 159.

55 Gleeson, BJ (2010) *Lifeboat Cities*. University of New South Wales Press, Sydney, p. 104.
56 Ibid, p. 142.
57 Descartes, R (1953) 'Les passions de l'ame', in Bridoux, A (ed.), *Oeuvres et lettres*, Gallimard, Paris, p. 166.
58 Gros, F (2019) *The Security Principle*, Verso, London, p. 186.
59 Benjamin, W (2002) *The Arcades Project*, translated by Eiland, H and Mcloughlin, K, Harvard University Press, Cambridge, MA.
60 Ibid. p. 187.
61 Huysmans, J (2002) 'Defining Social Constructivism in Security Studies: The Normative Dilemma of Writing Security', *Alternatives*, 27: 47.
62 George W Bush, post 9/11 ' "For Us or Against Us" speech', accessed on www.history.com/topics/21st-century/war-on-terror-timeline
63 Buzan, B, Wæver, O, and de Wilde, J (1998). *Security. A New Framework for Analysis*, Rienner, London.
64 Williams, M (2003) 'Words, Images, Enemies: Securitization and International Politics', *International Studies Quarterly*, 47: 518.
65 Steele, W, Hussey, K and Dovers, S (2017) What's Critical about Critical Infrastructure? *Urban Policy and Research*, 35 (1): 74–86.
66 Floyd, R (2007) 'Towards a Consequentialist Evaluation of Security: Bringing Together the Copenhagen and the Welsh Schools of Security Studies', *Review of International Studies*, 33: 327–50.
67 Eckersley, R (2004) *The Green State: Rethinking Democracy and Sovereignty*, MIT Press, Cambridge, MA, p. 256.
68 Dovers, S and Handmer, J (2014) 'Disaster Policy and Climate Change: How Much More of the Same?', in Ismail-Zadeh, A, Urrutia-Fucugaughi, J, Kijko, A, Takeuchi, K, and Zaliapin, I (eds), *Extreme Natural Hazards, Disaster Risks and Societal Implications*. Cambridge University Press, Cambridge, pp. 348–58.

Reflections from Wilderness (Photographer: Russell Blamey)

4 Seeking the good city

Lost horizon

The 1933 novel by English writer James Hilton, *Lost Horizon*, is best known for its depiction of a fictional place he named Shangri-La: an earthly paradise or holy grail that is always sought after but never found. Hilton imagined a Tibetan-style valley and monastery far from the modern Western world. The horizon is described variously in the dictionary as the line at which the earth's surface and the sky appear to meet; the limit of a person's knowledge, experience, or interest; or as in archaeology, a level of an excavated site representing a particular period.[1]

Thirty years later, Shangri-La became the title of a hit single by the English band The Kinks on their album *Arthur (or the Decline and Fall of the British Empire)*. The inspiration came from the Adelaide suburb of Elizabeth in Australia where the band performed a show in 1964. Band members and brothers Ray and Dave Davies visited their sister, who had married an Australian, and played a concert. The family lived in a semi-detached home in a new planned community, which became the inspiration for the song lyrics and a satirical twist on the vision of the good life in the city as paradise – a suburban Shangri-La after working so hard.[2]

Thirty years later again, and the modest town of Elizabeth in Adelaide, South Australia, appears again in a 1992 report entitled 'Planning the Good City in Australia: Elizabeth as a New Town', by Mark Peel of the Urban Research Program at the Australian National University. As a nice segue to the themes of The Kinks music around post-war disillusionment, Peel argues the development of the planned new town of Elizabeth reflected the post-war British town planning movement, which dominated Australian planning. 'Planners expected, and located, a morality in industrial capitalism, a commitment to the good city in the good society.'[3]

Town planners assumed that through the proper organization of space, working-class residents could be 'improved' and businesses would conform to the good city vision of 'a cohesive and mixed community' and 'a harmonious as well as profitable landscape'. This was an expert-led planning intervention intended to deliver a socially balanced and diverse community, and capitalist ventures that were efficient and productive. Good planning would deliver the good city for working communities in terms of community cohesions and productive enterprise. But there were problems.

> The building of the city reflected the difficulty of implementing borrowed templates for the 'good city', especially in terms of 'self-containment' and 'social mix'. Increasingly wary of the unauthorised activities of residents and doubtful about the means of creating … the officials began to rely heavily on employers to guarantee the social as well as economic outcomes of the project.[4]

The planning ideology behind the new town of Elizabeth was a vision of a better urban society for a working-class and migrant community on the urban fringe. This included cheap housing, community facilities, and a reduction in urban sprawl. With the downturn of the economy in the 1970s, the planned approach to city betterment as ideological and technical determinism began to fracture and falter through increased poverty and social alienation.

Peel concludes that it was not in the end the failure of the planners or the community that prevented the good city from being delivered as promised.

> The real message of Elizabeth is not what went wrong with planning, but what happens to good intentions and model communities in a society which must always push the costs of eventual crisis onto those with the fewest resources, whether they live in a new town or an old slum.[5]

As the Shangri-La lyrics by The Kinks highlight the insecurity of suburban life on the fringe, the mythical paradise of 'the good life' is kept dangling with the promise of new commodities, but always just out of reach.

The Western tradition of city planning was born of a vision of 'the good city'. Its roots lie in urban progressive reform that sought to bring order to the nineteenth-century industrial city. 'Their common purpose was to achieve efficiency, order, and beauty through the imposition of reason.'[6] In practice, this involved identifying and implementing models of the good city at the neighbourhood or metropolitan scale such as the planned new town of Elizabeth. But should visionaries impose their views upon the public? Is it possible to identify a model good city?

The early thinking around the good city is often linked to the teachings of Aristotle around the attainment of the 'good life'. What constitutes this 'good life' is described by Aristotle as *eudaimonia* – flourishing or happiness. This is the pursuit of human flourishing through ideals and action infused by reason and moral virtue; the rational pursuit of what is worthwhile in life through ethical activity and contemplation, rather than material wealth and power. For Aristotle, human flourishing is the quest for the moral life of virtue through which human beings attain happiness, success, and well-being.[7]

Aristotle's idea of the good life was explicitly linked to the city-state (the polis) in which individuals operate within social groupings of settlements and communities. Aristotle emphasizes the *synoikismos* or the amalgamation of villages into a city-state or polis within which 'a state is not a mere society, having a common place, established for the prevention of mutual crime and for the sake of exchange', but instead 'a community of families and aggregations of families in well-being, for the sake of a perfect and self-sufficing life'.[8]

This necessitates active participation in urban affairs to secure life's necessities and promote citizen happiness as part of the broader civic polity. The collective and civic-minded city is thus greater than the sum of its individual citizenry parts, but all are important. This is because 'the goodness' of the city-state is directly linked to the prospects and possibilities for 'the goodness' of the individuals who inhabit it. The sum and its parts are all equally important.

Urban planning theorist John Friedmann similarly argued that the good city requires an intentional civic politics. His focus was on human flourishing as a human right, which the good city must foster and enhance through ongoing discourse intended to encourage progressive urban possibility and solidarity in practice. He offered three key imaginings of the good city, but also some key critical questions that underpin these imaginings.

- Whose city are we talking about? (Can we legitimately assume the possibility of a collective idea of the good city?)
- Are we concerned only with process or only with outcomes – or should outcome and process be considered jointly?

• How can the good city framework be put to work in planning practice?[9]

His argument is that there must be a common-good agenda to establishing those minimal conditions for the good city – political, economic, social, physical, and ecological – which are necessary for human flourishing. But the good life is in the detail. There must be an emphasis on both process and outcome for this to be realized. The aspirations of the good city must extend to everyday practices – connected and responsible – with good governance attentive to civic participation and the way decisions are made and carried out, by whom and for whom.

Sceptics and critics point to the chimerical quality of the 'good city' as planning's holy grail – constantly sought in principle and never achieved in practice. In part this is because just what constitutes the good city is deeply contested depending on your politics and perspective. Urban theorist Susan Fainstein argues that the progressive/leftist ideal of a revitalized, cosmopolitan, just and democratic city remains defined in terms of democracy, equity, diversity, growth, and sustainability. These values, she argues, however, 'are problematic in that they all have undesirable potentials or risks'.[10]

There is an assumption that what is good for a city and its citizens, or even what is bad, are clearly understood values and agreed upon principles. This is rarely, if ever, the case. The 'just' city is only one vision jostling for space amongst many competing 'good' city models that may include, but are by no means limited to, the neoliberal city, the future city, the smart city, the ordinary city, the city of diversity, the resilient city, the green city, the post-colonial city, or the zero-carbon city. Which version you support will depend on what you seek to see flourish.

In a climate of change, the good city seems distant and utopian – a lost urban horizon.

The urban pulse

However weakly the urban pulse is beating, the quest for the good city is persistent, particularly within planning. Urban social theorist Richard Sennett believes the good city can be attained as an ethic of craftsmanship and modesty. The good city is about making the connections between how people live and what is being built – and for whom. The good city is imagined as much about the *process* as the *outcomes* of metropolitan craft building: one that makes the connections with the equity dimensions of urban life.[11] The good city is thus linked to the good life and human flourishing, and is a response to the civic question, 'how ought we to live?'

Cities as sites of thriving community and well-being; creativity driven by global circulation and trans-local connectivity; good citizenship, good government, and a robust public sphere; urban proximity that locates difference and heterogeneity together; and the spatial juxtaposition of 'strangers, strangeness and continuous change' as part of the processes of urban encounter.

These are all part of the premise upon which urban geographer Ash Amin bases his urban ethic. Exactly what constitutes the good city will emerge in response to the circumstances of the times. As Amin notes, 'The concept of good does not track unmodified across space and time.' He asks, 'Can the contemporary city qualify as the good life?'[12]

The good city as a 'pragmatism of the possible' is levelled at the fine-grain of human experience – practice, place and circumstance – to create transformative urban change. For cities to realize a politics of well-being and emancipation – the good life – Amin argues four necessary registers of *repair, relatedness, rights* and *re-enchantment* must infuse the urban weave. Through these four registers he invites us to re-think the idea of the good city as 'a challenge to forge a progressive politics of well-being and emancipation out of the urban experience', and asks 'how can care become the filter of urban experience?'[13]

Repair

The good city commits to accessible and affordable shelter, sanitation, sustenance, water, communication and mobility for the survival and well-being of its citizens. A focus on the politics of 'repair' is to expose and address the urban machinery and intelligence that forms the life-support system of cities. These infrastructural worlds are underpinned by powerful processes and vested interests. Making visible the socio-technical spaces of cities is an important way of inserting an alternative weave of technology and the social into the urban fabric. 'Infrastructure disruptions radically transform urban life as urbanites seek to adjust and cope with uncanny worlds of darkness, cold, immobility, hunger, thirst or dirt. Often the sense of crisis and the search for alternatives helps to forge new ideas about what urban life might be.'[14]

Relatedness

The good city is the socially just city, with a strong obligation towards human rights and solidarity with, and for, other citizens. Amin describes this as 'a duty of care towards the insider and the outsider' regardless of ethnicity, race, gender, age, or ability, including migrants, the homeless, and the itinerant.[15] This includes, for example, a commitment to security, healthcare, education, housing and employment. A politics of relatedness is a necessary counterpoint to the disconnection and disenchantment that arises through processes of segregation and alienation in both public and private life. Access to public space for interaction is as important as public institutions, movements, and commons (physical and virtual), creating spaces 'where strangers meet'[16] and opportunities for encounter in cities of difference in ways that are transformative rather than aggressive or regressive.

Rights

The good city is intimately linked to the citizen's right to shape and benefit from urban life.[17] In *The Culture of Cities* by Sharon Zukin, this is described as 'finding a home in the city'– for the many not just the few.[18] Can the disempowered stake a claim? Can new voices emerge and be heard? Can dissent sit with democracy? These are some of the key questions that underpin a politics of rights as one of the four registers of an urban ethic of solidarity. In doing so, the good city stands in contrast to both the city of majority mob rule, fear, and violence, and the city of elite prejudicial violence. Amin talks of the need for an 'open' civic culture that upholds rights by working with difference and disagreement. This serves to 'expose its [urban] wrongs as well as reveal alternatives rooted in a habit of solidarity'.[19]

Re-enchantment

Finally, the good city is a politics of re-enchantment, described by Amin as another register of solidarity. Rather than urban utopia, this is envisaged as urban sociality and gathering in public spaces. The vitality of these civic public spaces of the city acts as a visible gauge for the health, engagement and conviviality of the urban realm. As he describes:

> The sites I have in mind are the associations, clubs, car-boot sales, restaurants, open spaces, bolt-holes, libraries, formal and informal gathering places, and multitude of friendship circles that so fill

cities. These sites form an essential component of the urban public culture and are an important filter through which urban life is judged as a collective social good.[20]

This civic sociality is seen as a counterpoint to commodification and homogenization of the city on the one hand and disinterested and disengaged individualism on the other. This is expressed through experimental everyday public space through art, performance, protest, celebration, gatherings – performative expressions of public cultural solidarity. This is imagined as 'an ever-widening habit of solidarity built around different dimensions of the urban common weal'.[21]

The good city is a collective task of urban solidarity, 'a politics of small gains and fragile truces that constantly need to be worked at, but which can add up, with resonances capable of binding difference as well as reining in the powerful and the abusive'.[22] This is the self-organizing community and empowered neighbourhoods, deeply committed to the collective responsibilities of a civil urban society.

But the word 'community' is no simple antidote, holding many conflicting meanings. Whilst it conjures up utopian and idealistic views of how the good society functions, fundamental equity questions about who is recognized and who has access to information, resources, and power can be dismissed or sidelined. The idea of community can divide and exclude people as much as it might include and support them. All communities contain 'fault-lines', which can open up in times of stress or disturbance,[23] undermining the central tenets and notions of the good city.

Accelerating mobility means that a sense of belonging to community has become more fleeting and fragile than it has in earlier times. Increasing global flows of people, goods, information, and ideas have added even more layers of meaning to the word community. New forms of citizenship range from place-based 'local' communities to 'virtual', spatially extended networks and 'imagined' communities of people who may never have contact with each other. Far from being fixed and static, the concept of community is on the move as both a socio-spatial construction and human aspiration – and not all contemporary manifestations support and promote human solidarity and flourishment.

The good enough city?

The twenty-first century has ushered in the idea of the 'good enough' city. This is a response to the moral determinism around what constitutes 'good' as a fixed end point or destination for cities. It is also a reminder that an important prerequisite to cities being good, is their capacity to exist at all in the face of the catastrophic impacts of climate change. Urban geographer Brendan Gleeson, for example, describes human history as a 'species journey' in the face of potentially catastrophic social and environmental change. He compares humanity to the pilgrim ever-seeking the path to the good – in this case the long march to the good (enough) city as a central and compelling view of human improvement and prospect.[24]

In part, this is a critique of the vision for cities as sites of accumulation, power, and capital, rather than as habitats driven by a deep ethic of individual and civic responsibility. But this is also a signal to what the good city might mean in the face of threatened species survival. Pushed to this extreme, is the good city simply the survival of the city and its inhabitants no matter the cost? Or, as Gleeson argues, far greater recognition that 'the city is simultaneously our principal act of realization, and our greatest disturbance of the natural order'. This city will require a different kind of ethic and solidarity that goes far beyond just settlement resilience.

The good enough city argument can be extended to our engagement with technology. The 'smart enough' city proposed by scientist Ben Green, for example, is a practical utopian ambition that seeks to restore the balance between technology, justice, and equity, and not just value the pursuit of technology as the ultimate end in and of itself. The smart enough city asks the question: smart enough for what?[25] This shifts the focus of technology to be a means to achieve progressive ends.

This question can be replicated across other contemporary urban utopias as a critical heuristic, with numerous examples, such as the creative city: creative enough for what? The resilient city: resilient enough for what? Or liveable cities: liveable enough for what? The slow city: slow enough for what? In the face of globalization, climate change, and the growing energy crisis, the slow movement, for example, has been gaining grassroots popular ascendancy as a diverse form of resistance to the pace and principles underpinning the dominant thrust of economic, social, and cultural practice/s.

Natural philosopher Daniel Milo argues that optimization and innovation as part of the quest for 'good' have become dangerously overrated: that 'imperfection is not just good enough, it may at times be essential to survival'. In a Darwinian sense, he asks rhetorically, 'Why should we struggle and strain when we are already good enough?'[26]

We face no species level threat except perhaps those ecological ones that are products of unavoidable excess. This excess is unavoidable because we have little to do from a survival standpoint. Humans have the ultimate luxury of wasting time and resources in order to divert ourselves ... Our excess bubbles and blooms not because it is selected through a process of struggle, but because there is no struggle.[27]

Milo's hypothesis is that the capacity to keep inventing the future is the key to human longevity. The ability to project ourselves into the future and creatively re-imagine ourselves and our habitats is unique to *Homo urbanis*. 'Humanity bends to the dream of tomorrow and the change it portends, enabling all our species brilliance and all its waste.'[28] And so it is with our cities.

Future cities

In Australia, two future city initiatives are instructive and will be briefly outlined. First is the 1987 *Multifunction Polis (MFP)*, a joint venture initiated by the Australian and Japanese governments to build 'a city of dreams'. The MFP was envisaged as a high-tech city of the future, with futuristic infrastructure, nuclear power, modern communication and Asian investment – a 'brave new world' concept of a future city where work and leisure, lifetime education and intercultural exchange, research and manufacturing would blossom. It was never built, unable to leverage the necessary political, investment and public support needed.

Three concepts drove the MFP: a biosphere to address ecological problems; a technopolis to develop innovative technology; and a renaissance polis to support international arts, culture and research. By 1997, the MFP was replaced by a more conventional technology park and industrial urban development. 'The MFP has finally landed. What began life as a sci-fi Japanese satellite techno-city turns out to be something much less sinister – a friendly village-style housing development with a comfortable green, technological edge.'[29]

Thirty years later, it is mainly the *technopolis agenda* that is driving the current *CLARA Plan*, which proposes building up to eight smart new regional cities connected by a high-speed rail system linking Sydney and Melbourne via Canberra. Each of the new cities is designed to be compact, environmentally sustainable, and within close proximity to the capital cities along the proposed rail corridor. CLARA has the land for new city development and has outlined a land value capture business model based on private city development, not 'government coffer', funding. The argument put forward by the CLARA project is that

> city planners need to embrace a less homogenous and prescriptive planning framework which create 'activity silos' which in turn creates reliance on cars ... By creating well planned, mixed-use precincts and intensifying the use of existing infrastructure and new infrastructure a more effective and ambitious planning outcome can be achieved.[30]

Emphasis has been placed on articulating the funding, technological, and lifestyle benefits of the project.

Curiously little has been put into place as to how these new cities will function as a democratic polity, urban governance, and planning agenda within the constitutional framework of Australia. Striking the balance between innovative new ideas and democratic expectations around the public right to the city is yet to be resolved in relation to Australia's future cities.

The Minnesota Experimental City in the United States offers a cautionary tale about the implementation of futuristic cities planned to be built from scratch. The ambition was to solve urban problems through the latest technology (including nuclear energy, automated cars, and a domed roof enclosure) to create the most liveable city. Despite significant government and financial backing, including the development of its own state agency, the project failed due to lack of public support and a clear understanding of the democratic and political implications of top-down projects, no matter how creative.

In a literal and metaphorical sense, 'future city' thinking is shifting the twenty-first-century urban imaginary around what is possible in a climate of growth-led change. Whereas cities were once seen as the locus of the problem in terms of crime, sprawl, congestion, poverty, social alienation, slums and pollution, amongst other things, they are now viewed as beacons of possibility for furthering economic, democratic, and sustainability goals.

New cities that are smart, green, low-carbon, and energy efficient are being designed and built from scratch, drawing on new technologies, funding models, and critical infrastructure. The United States, India, China, Africa, Malaysia, Sri Lanka, Oman, and Saudi Arabia, to name a few, have all signalled their intention to build new cities focusing on sustainable development initiatives such as carless and walkable cities; green cities that produce oxygen through eco-skyscrapers; smart cities with high-speed internet embedded in the urban fabric; waste converted into energy; and new city development on reclaimed land increasing strategic port and trade positioning.

A different logic can be applied if the critical question for the good city is: good enough for what? The challenge is to be able to both 'stay with the trouble' of human hubris, excess and activity, and at the same time not retreat from imagining alternatives and the possibility of better worlds.

Staying with the trouble

What then, is the role of utopian visions of the future city today? Can visions of the good city meet the needs and complexities of contemporary times? The literature on urban utopias might be productive here in countering the cul-de-sac thinking that pervades, indeed defines, the hauntology of the Anthropocene. Utopian thinking offers a break with historical continuity; a creative imaginary not held back by the dominant politics of the day; the ability to think of alternatives to the present as a necessary precondition of change.

Utopian thinking – as opposed to grand project utopian visions of the twentieth and twenty-first centuries – offers the capacity 'to imagine a future that departs significantly from what we know to be a general condition in the present', and 'may alert us to certain tendencies in the present, which, if allowed to continue unchecked and carried to a logical extreme, would result in a world we would find abhorrent'.[31] Interrogating the political, economic, sociocultural, and ecological contours of utopian thinking raises 'profound questions about "the city" as an object of analysis and also about the future expression of citizenship, spatial justice and urban politics'.[32]

Despite this there has been a retreat – even abandonment – of utopian urbanism as a useful response to the challenges of cities and the urban question. The quest for the good city has been critiqued for being too moralistic, narrow, authoritarian, determi025tic, and inherently unattainable.

> We have grown used to looking at Utopia only to discover that we have created Hell.[33]

Many of the twentieth-century planning attempts to build ideal cities and societies have created more problems than they have solved in their efforts to remake urban space and experience, and mould it to a particular vision. 'Utopian thinking about cities has rarely produced anything other than misty-eyed simplisms that have failed to engender transformative change.'[34] As Marxist urban geographer David Harvey pessimistically notes, 'To talk of the city of the twenty-first century is to conjure up a dystopian nightmare in which all that is judged worst in the fatally flawed character of humanity collects together in some hell-hole of despair.'[35]

Yet despite the challenges of climate change, economic precarity and a widening social equity divide, utopian thinking and action remains. Reimagining the future city is still relevant and vital for building the progressive cities yet to come. However, there have been calls for a shift away from urban utopias that privilege a fixed state or form of the good city model. The last century has ushered in – nay poked, prodded and insisted on – more open, plural, and disruptive ways of imagining the future.

To this end, urban geographer David Pinder calls for what he describes as an oppositional utopianism that seeks to trace alternative possibilities for what cities might become. This includes critical engagement with the current complexities of urban spaces and processes in the name of a better future. This analysis of current conditions and crises is made in light of the possibilities and potentialities of the common good, with radical and social rather than technical or managerial change at the core. The critique of the present is thus simultaneously a look into the future and the conduit for the types of urban transformation that it aims to encourage.[36]

The future city Pinder describes 'can thus be subversive, stimulating demands for action and political practice, exploring how things might be different'.[37] Imagining cities without utopia is 'the imagination of the absence', including the collective consciousness of 'what is missing, forbidden and hidden, and yet possible, in modern life'.[38] It is precisely the potentially disruptive and dialectical qualities of urban utopianism that hold the possibility for transformation.

> There is a need for forms of utopian urbanism that work to challenge, to estrange taken-for-granted assumptions about the organisation of space and time, to interrupt dominant conceptions about linear temporal progression or good spatial form in the effort to open up unrealised possibilities in the present ... wary of the danger of longing for singular pictures of the future or for supposedly stable and adequate representations of a 'good society'... Instead, this approach allows a more open conception

of utopianism that is transformative in intent and that connects with other currents of critical contemporary utopianism.[39]

French philosopher and urbanist Henri Lefebvre describes this as a 'philosophy of the possible',[40] and alongside feminist, Indigenous, queer, and other theorists, this approach has been grounded in the struggle and creative disruption, which are part of the process, rather than some finalized blue-print destination. This has been described as 'an approach toward, a movement beyond set limits into the realm of the not-yet-set',[41] or what planning theorist Leonie Sandercock labels 'Utopia in the becoming', a cosmopolis that is envisaged not as a state to be realized, but as a movement constantly open to change and contestation.

The work of Marxist philosopher Ernst Bloch in *The Principle of Hope* explores the ways in which everyday activities could embody the practical utopian impulse.[42] For David Harvey, this is about imagination and political guts: a dialectical urbanism that is both grounded in the possibilities of the present and pointing towards trajectories of the future. This 'emancipatory politics calls for a living Utopianism of process as opposed to the dead Utopianism of spatialized urban form ... an attentiveness to the dialectic between "process" and "thing", between urbanization and cities, as a focus for struggle'.[43]

The act of disruption is how critical geographer Donna Haraway describes the word 'trouble', but for different purposes. She cautions against reacting to the trouble by pinning hopes on an imagined perfect future safely decoupled from the past and present. Instead, she argues we should 'stay with the trouble of living and dying in response-ability on a damaged earth'.[44] The meaning of trouble is three-fold: we live in troubling times, 'turbid, mixed up and disturbing'; we need to make trouble and 'stir up a potent response to devastating events'; and we need to then settle the troubled waters through the rebuilding of quiet places.

Haraway invokes speculative feminism, science fiction, science, and what she describes as 'string figures' amongst other tools for teasing out threads and finding tangles and patterns in particular contexts, times, places, and spaces. Living, she argues, requires:

> ... learning to be truly present, not as a vanishing pivot between awful or edenic pasts and apocalyptic or salvific futures, but as mortal critters entwined in myriad unfinished configurations of places, times, matters and meanings.[45]

Like Harvey, this is about imagination and guts, about both practice and process and 'becoming-with' each other in an entangled weave
of on-going-ness. Unlike Harvey, her ambition is not the dialectic of
despair and hope, but instead a turn to the counter-weave of the
mindful, the material, and the senses, which are always, she argues,
situated someplace not no place as abstract futurism tends to be. The
response to climate change is neither retreat to humanism nor futurism – instead we need to stay with the trouble.

This would appear to be a stake in the utopian heart. Where does
that leave the good city?

The swing of the pendulum

Cities shape us and we shape them, but in what ways? The idea of the
good city is for many an imagined response to the philosophical question, 'how ought we to live?' This is about means (instruments or
actions for living and achieving the good life) and ends (that which is
useful to people for human flourishment). The quest for the good city
is described as an elusive, mystical object or lived experience that is
constantly sought after but rarely attained – a highly desired but prac-
tically unobtainable prize.[46] As Lesley Head highlights in her book
Hope and Grief in the Anthropocene:

> Hope is a risky and complex process of possibility that carries
> painful emotions; it is something to be practised rather than felt.
> As centralised governmental solutions regarding climate change
> appear insufficient, intellectual and practical resources can be
> derived from everyday understandings and practices.[47]

Australian geographer Natalie Osbourne writes, with resonance to
Donna Haraway's urge to stay with the trouble, of the need to maintain hope for the 'still possible worlds' yet to come: there *are* still possible worlds, still possible shared futures, still possible cities, and
some of them are worth having.[48]

Both the idea and the ideal of the good city have served as light-
house beacon and moral compass for Western cities of the global
north, particularly for philosophers, writers, and academics – arguably less so for the citizens most definitions of the good city purport
to serve. The good city implies a good set of principles around the
question, 'how ought we to live?' This is namely around commitment to the common good, robust civic engagement, open and inclusive processes, justice, and equity amongst diverse and shifting

communities. There is also recognition that what this looks like will be different for different physical and cultural contexts and social settings, and that the process is as important as the outcome in city-making. Building and dwelling is how Richard Sennett describes the two interconnected urban crafts.

Resistance to the good city ideal has come from many. The first is a reaction to what is concealed within this moral quest for the good city. Good for whom? Good when? Good for what? Who gets to decide what is good or even good enough? Who is the 'we' in 'how ought we to live'? The wealthy, white people, men, human species? And if the good city is an unattainable utopia, how does this usefully assist with navigating the past or the present with purpose? The practical utopians reject abstract futurism and the quest for a 'perfect city' for a more grounded and interconnected vision around the joined-up moments of urban critique and construction. Harvey, for example, calls for imagination and political guts to take us there.

Equally problematic is the notion that within the context of climate change, 'the good life' is still the appropriate ambition. Many would argue it is this human-centred idea of the good life that has led to the current ecological and social crisis. What does the good city mean in a world that is no longer able to support the biodiversity of life itself? Can we conceive of a good city citadel surrounded by species extinction and biodiversity degradation? Is this the return of the walled city on the hill, separate and bounded away from other forms of life? The city is but a moment in a wider urban context that is deeply interconnected with the hinterlands – urban or other – but is this what is imagined in the idea of the good city?

If not the good city, then what? Haraway's offering of 'staying with the trouble' urges grounded and imaginative re-engagement with the world as a deeply entangled human and other-than-human habitat. Rather than quests for other worlds, this involves being truly present to effectively respond to the challenges of the Anthropocene and capital, including the idea that 'we have lost'. Alternately depressing, therapeutic, mobilizing, and motivating, other philosophers and activists write of the age of hopelessness as the necessary precursor to action.

Clive Hamilton's *Requiem for a Species*, for example, argues we need to accept the failure of climate action in order to move forward, similar to the grieving process required for moving on after a death of a loved one. Similarly, radical philosopher Slavoj Žižek describes true courage as not accepting alternatives but instead accepting the consequences that there is no alternative. He argues:

The dream of an alternative is a sign of theoretical cowardice, functioning as a fetish that prevents us from thinking through to the end the deadlock of our predicament. In short true courage is to admit that the light at the end of the tunnel is probably the headlight of another train approaching us from the other direction.[49]

This train takes many forms, most recently capitalism and climate change. To this we might add cities. The 'courage of hopelessness' resists the avoidance of risks through careful attentiveness and the making of right choices, but instead to be 'fully aware of the explosive set of interconnections that makes the entire situation dangerous'.[50] Once we do this we can begin the long journey of recalibrating the coordinates of the entire situation.

Philosopher Hannah Arendt similarly claimed that the burden of our time must 'be faced without a bannister' and only by reappropriating through new thoughts can we seek to restore meaning to the present and shine light on the contemporary context and experience.[51] By contrast, writer Rebecca Solnit suggests we can carve out hope in the dark. Hope is not, she argues, the belief that everything will be fine, but that hope and grief can co-exist amidst the rise of new forms of resistance building in the shadows and margins of the status quo.[52] As Osbourne speculates, despite losing the war, there are still possible worlds to come:

In fact, we lost that battle, lost that future, lost that world.
We. Have. *Lost*.
Take a breath.
Now what?[53]

So, let us assume for a moment, that the quest for seeking the good city has largely failed. That in holding on too tightly, or not tightly enough, to the good city ideal and its alternatives (i.e. the good enough city), we have lost more ground than we gained. We have avoided the root and branch re-assessment of city thinking that is needed in this climate of change.

As writer Maria Tumarkin observes in *Axiomatic*,

The past shapes the present (Shapes? Infiltrates more like, imbues, infuses). This past cannot be visited like an aging aunt. It doesn't live in little zoo enclosures. Half the time, the past is nothing less than the present's beating heart. How to speak of its aliveness? Stories are not enough, history and psychology – not enough. Maybe this is how.[54]

The swing of the pendulum returns us to the idea of the wild city – to be re-thought and re-tasked to the contemporary moment and purpose. But to do this requires first exploring the framing of the wild city that is currently positioned within, and in contrast to, the good city narrative. Good for whom, when, and how, by what means? And then do the necessary disruptive work to change this.

For we are the wild city. The present's beating heart. How to speak of its aliveness?

Maybe this is how.

Notes

1 Oxford (2019) accessed on www.lexico.com/en/definition/horizon
2 Hinman, D (2004) *The Kinks: All Day and All of the Night.* Backbeat Books, Lanham, MD. pp. 144–62.
3 See Duff, A (1961) *Britain's New Towns: An Experiment in Living*, London, pp. 61–5; Purdom, C (1949) *The Building of Satellite Towns: A Contribution to the Study of Town Development and Regional Planning*, 2nd ed., London, pp. 267–80.
4 Peel, M (1992) 'Planning the Good city in Australia: Elizabeth as a New Town', in Coles, R (ed.), Urban Research Program Working Paper No. 30, February, Australian National University, Canberra.
5 Ibid., p. 35.
6 Fainstein, S (2006) *Planning and the Just City*, paper presented at the Conference on Searching for the Just City, GSAPP Columbia University, Columbia, April 29, p. 1.
7 Youngkins, E (2003) *Aristotle, Human Flourishing and the Limited State*, Le Quebecois Libre, accessed on www.quebecoislibre.org/031122-11.htm
8 Lane, M (2018) 'Ancient Political Philosophy', *The Stanford Encyclopedia of Philosophy* (Winter Edition), accessed on https://plato.stanford.edu/entries/ancient-political/
9 Friedmann, J (2000) 'The Good City: In Defense of Utopian Thinking', *International Journal of Urban and Regional Research*, 24(2): 460–72.
10 Fainstein, S (2006) *Planning and the Just City*, paper presented at the Conference on Searching for the Just City, GSAPP Columbia University, Columbia, April 29, p. 3.
11 Sennett, R (2008) *The Craftsman*, Yale University Press, London; Sennet, R (2018) *Building and Dwelling: Ethics for the City*, Penguin, London.
12 Amin, A (2006) 'The Good City', *Urban Studies*, 43(5/6): 1009–23.
13 Ibid.
14 Graham, S (2010) *Disrupted Cities: When Infrastructure Fails*, Routledge, London, p. xi.
15 Amin, A (2006) 'The Good City', *Urban Studies*, 43(5/6): 1009–23.
16 Sandercock, L (2000) 'When Strangers Become Neighbours: Managing Cities of Difference', *Planning Theory and Practice*, 1(1): 13–30.
17 Lefebvre, H (1996) *Writings on Cities*, trans. and ed. by E. Kofman and E. Lebas. Oxford: Blackwell.
18 Zukin, S. (1996) *The Cultures of Cities*, Blackwell, Oxford.

19 Amin, A (2006) 'The Good City', *Urban Studies*, 43(5/6): 1009–23.
20 Ibid., p. 1009.
21 Ibid., p. 1013.
22 Ibid., p. 1019.
23 Mulligan, M (2015) 'On Ambivalence and Hope in the Restless Search for Community: How to Work with the Idea of Community in the Global Age', *Sociology*, 49: 2, pp. 340–55.
24 Gleeson, B (2010) *Lifeboat Cities*, UNSW Press, Sydney, p. 192.
25 Green, B (2019) *The Smart Enough City: Putting Technology in its Place to Reclaim our Urban Future*, MIT Press, Cambridge, MA.
26 Milo, D (2019) *Good Enough-the Tolerance for Mediocrity in Nature and Society*, Harvard University Press, Cambridge, MA, p. 24.
27 Ibid.
28 Ibid., p. 189.
29 The Advertiser (1996) 'The Friendly City: Smart it May Be, but Friendly is the Operative Word for the Proposed Multifunction Polis', 30 October p. 17, cited in Parker, P (1998) *The Multifunction Polis 1987–97: An International Failure or Innovative Local Project?* Pacific Economic Paper No. 283, Australia-Japan Research centre, Crawford School, ANU, Canberra.
30 CLARA Plan (2018) accessed on www.clara.com.au/the-clara-plan.html
31 Friedmann, J (2000) 'The Good City: In Defense of Utopian Thinking', *International Journal of Urban and Regional Research*, 24(2): 462.
32 MacLeod, G and Ward, K (2002) 'Spaces of Utopia and Dystopia: Landscaping the Contemporary City', *Geografiska Annaler. Series B, Human Geography*, 84(3/4): 153, 153–70.
33 Raban, J. (1988) *Soft City*. Collins Harvill, London.
34 Gleeson, B (2019) 'Seeking the Good (Enough) City', in Bohland, J, Davoudi, S and Lawrence, J (eds.), *The Resilience Machine*, Routledge, New York, p. 184.
35 Harvey, D (2000) *Spaces of Hope*, University of Edinburgh Press, Edinburgh.
36 Benhabib, S (1986) *Critique, Norm and Utopia: A Study of the Foundations of Critical Theory*, Columbia University Press, New York, 225–7.
37 Pinder, D (2002) 'In Defence of Utopian Urbanism: Imagining Cities after the "End of Utopia"', *Geografiska Annaler. Series B, Human Geography*, 84 (3/4): 229–41. Special Issue: The Dialectics of Utopia and Dystopia (2002).
38 Ibid., p. 238.
39 Ibid.
40 Lefebvre, H (1996) *Writings on Cities*, trans. and ed. by E. Kofman and E. Lebas. Oxford: Blackwell, p. 348.
41 Bammer, A (1991) *Partial Visions: Feminism and Utopianism in the 1970s*, Routledge, London, p. 7; Sargisson, L (2000) *Contemporary Feminist Utopianism*, Routledge, London.
42 Bloch, E (1986) *The Principle of Hope*, MIT Press, Cambridge, MA.
43 Harvey, D (2000) *Spaces of Hope*, University of Edinburgh Press, Edinburgh. p. 187.
44 Haraway, DJ (2016) *Staying with the Trouble: Making Kin in the Chthulucene*, Duke University Press, Durham, NC.
45 Ibid., p. 1.
46 Ibid.

47 Head, L (2016) *Hope and Grief in the Anthropocene: Reconceptualizing Human-nature Relations*, Routledge, London.
48 Osbourne, N (2019) 'For Still Possible Cities: A Politics of Failure for the Politically Depressed', in *Australian Geographer*, 50(2): 145–54.
49 Žižek, S (2017) *The Courage of Hopelessness: Chronicles of a Year of Acting Dangerously*, Penguin, London.
50 Ibid., p. xi.
51 Arendt, H (1958) *The Human Condition*, University of Chicago Press, Chicago.
52 Solnit, R (2016) *Hope in the Dark: Untold Histories, Wild Possibilities*, Canongate Books, Edinburgh.
53 Osbourne, N (2019) 'For Still Possible Cities: A Politics of Failure for the Politically Depressed', *Australian Geographer*, 50(2): 145–54.
54 Tumarkin, M (2018) *Axiomatic*, Brow Books, Melbourne.

The Paddler (Artist: Michael Steele)

5 We are the wild city

The language of cities

If you search for the words 'wild cities' online, you will quickly come across the BBC2 website titled 'Cities: Natures New Wild'. The focus is on wild animals as outcasts of the urbanization process, pushed out of their homes and habitats as development multiplies across the globe. The message is hopeful, with examples of human–animal relationships that have been able to be forged, and in some cases even thrive in cities, given the right circumstances.

As narrator Sir David Attenborough pronounces in the final episode of the *Planet Earth II* series,

> Cities are growing at a faster rate than any other habitat on Earth. They may seem an unlikely place for animals to thrive but they can be worlds of surprising opportunities ... If we create the space, the animals will come. As the architects of this environment, can humans choose to build cities that are homes for both them and wildlife?[1]

The stewardship of nature in and around cities – particularly for wildlife – is part of a new language around cities, and why wild cities are the key to good urban health. Futuristic examples of city–nature interactions include the recently developed Gardens by the Bay in Central Singapore, which offers botanical gardens built on 100 hectares of reclaimed land. Within the gardens, 18 giant tree-like superstructures house solar panels and provide habitat for birds and animals, shade, and reflection of sunlight. This stewardship is also extended to include the capacity of nature to then better support urban happiness and well-being by building 'a city within a garden'[2] as part of the urban greening movement, which is growing globally.

This is the vision put forward by wildcities.org, which focuses on 'creating a world in which cities care for, and benefit from, healthy ecosystems'.[3] It is an initiative of the *Wild Foundation*, a not-for-profit organization focused on building strong communities that respect and protect nature for the benefit of all life. At a practical level, the emphasis is on urban wildlife and nature regeneration projects that promote the health benefits of wild nature for cities and citizens. Its motto is: 'If you believe in the importance of protecting Earth's wild and irreplaceable nature then you've come to the right place.'[4]

In Bristol and Bath in the United Kingdom, the Avon Wildlife Trust focuses its campaign efforts on engaging local community action. *My Wild City* seeks to recruit members to help re-imagine local urban habitats as spaces and places. In this way, 'whole streets and communities can get together to transform gardens and open spaces, from planting for pollinators in our gardens to influencing the space around us, we can all help to make a city better for people and wild-life'.[5] The emphasis is on bringing to the surface the hidden spaces and integrity of nature in the city, and in doing so the protection of the wildlife who exist within them (e.g. owls, badgers) in efforts to link communities to wildlife sites over the long term.

Back here in Australia, *Remember the Wild* is an organization dedicated to 'connecting people with nature and leading a positive shift in the way Australians value the natural world, for the benefit of both people and the environment'.[6] Its similar position is that modern life in cities is increasingly removed from nature and largely devoid of biodiversity and lived engagement with the natural world. Its ambition is to 'bring our experiences of the natural world back from the brink of extinction, reconnect our communities with nature, and help people remember why the wild matters'.[7] *Wild Melbourne* is the Victorian city hub for building a deeper appreciation of nature and the importance of experience and connection. Why?

> Because the world is beautiful. It is astonishingly complex and astoundingly diverse. Wild Melbourne seeks to educate people throughout Victoria so that they may be better equipped to understand and appreciate this world. In the face of pressures such as habitat fragmentation, overfishing, elevated greenhouse gas emissions and a soaring human population, our community needs to work together to ensure a healthy future for those who will inherit this beautiful world. This means working together to protect and preserve our native ecosystems, as ultimately it is the environment that underpins our economy and our health. Wild

Melbourne is dedicated to teaching members of our Victorian community about the natural world so that they may understand and come to appreciate it. We believe that with such an appreciation, our society may come to value and protect our environment for the sake of current and future generations.[8]

Within this context of care and community, it is a strangely surreal and somewhat unsettling experience to enter the Melbourne Museum Wild exhibit. There you can view more than 750 birds, reptiles, mammals, and amphibians located in their biogeographic regions, displayed as stuffed specimens in vertical array around the white walls of the museum. The exhibit seeks to showcase 'amazing animals in a changing world'. There is a vulnerability index for each animal so you can see by looking up the panoramic navigator if it is extinct, thriving, or just surviving – koalas, for example, as a result of the Australian bushfires.

The exhibition is visually spectacular in its diversity and arrangement and the emphasis is on species vulnerability and protection of habitat in climate change, including what you can do in your local area to preserve unique ecosystems. The role and impact of humans as both part of the problem and the solution is made clear. These animals are all stored, exhibited, and viewed within a room inside a building filled with artificial light.

The title of the exhibit 'Wild' seems so perversely detached and out of place. As you file past the taxidermic specimens with your friends and children, the species divide between 'us' and 'them' seems even more magnified in the white, air-conditioned sterility of the museum exhibition space. It makes you want to weep, and you probably do not even know why. After all, you, just like me, have probably at some time paid to enter a museum and view its exhibits. No one forced you. As in the ironic quote from the book *Fear and Loathing in Las Vegas*, we just 'Take the ticket and enjoy the ride'.[9]

A continuum between *domestic* nature and *wild* nature has been proposed by the authors of the edited book *The Rediscovery of the Wild*. Domestic nature is that which is part of the everyday urban experience – gardens, parks, trees, pigeons, dogs, cats, and the like. Wild nature, on the other hand, is contrasted as untamed, unmanaged, and unmediated by technology. This is based on the idea that 'as a species we came of age in a natural world far more wild than today and much of the need for wildness still exists within us, body and mind'.[10] The charter of their book is to bring forward the language of 'wild nature' so that we can both engage with what is left *and* try to recover what is being lost.

Neil Everneden describes this as 'the need for wild otherness' – where the unfamiliar can be encountered and multispecies possibilities can develop by retrieving some 'chaos' from nature. He suggests that what is needed for this wild otherness to flourish is 'a talent for speaking differently, rather than arguing well, as the chief instrument for cultural change'.[11] Although humanity appears to be largely alienated from nature, we can develop a new understanding of self in the wild and in doing so, in the world.[12]

In a paper entitled 'Urban Wild Things: A Cosmopolitical Experiment', geographer Steven Hinchcliffe and colleagues make the case for a politics for urban wilds, which sees urban living worlds as much more than simply human worlds, extending beyond the portal for human flourishment, enrichment, and the pursuit of the good life. Non-human, they argue, is not the same as nature or wilderness, and that we need to reach beyond 'crude maps and boundary markers' if we are to see progressive political struggle that fosters a wild urban polity. The term non-human they argue is important and signals

> a worldliness of worlds, suggesting that culture and societies are shaped by more-than-human geographies ... instead of human free choice versus the dead weight of matter we are interested instead in the fraught processes of engaging with human and non-human worlds.[13]

Hinchcliffe and his colleagues focus our attention on interstitial urban space, former industrial land that has been left vacant (for human use) but is now earmarked for redevelopment in the form of a new privately financed 'super' hospital. Over time, the site has become the habitat for multiple wildlife which make use of the patchwork corridors of abandoned urban land for habitats or passage. But the urban wilds in this context are largely disconnected from broader community dialogue around urban futures.

> ... the economic rationality of hi-tech corridors seems more at home than talk of wildlife corridors and other forms of ecological space ... not pure enough to be true and not human enough to be political, urban wilds have no constituency.[14]

Within environmental science and urban ecology, the language of 'rewilding' has provided a popular touchstone for conservation activities that seek to restore integrity to damaged environments by re-introducing species, attempting to revive extinct ones, or in the reconstruction of ecosystems. Rewilding exists

> because of the unprecedented rates of environmental change in the Anthropocene, which call for a paradigm shift from focusing on the preservation of individual species to the enhancement of ecosystem health and processes, and for new and pragmatic options for mitigating the degradation of biodiversity and eco-system services.[15]

In cities around the world, this has led to projects that focus on nature-based solutions, such as habitat corridors and revegetation, which are designed to deliver co-benefits for both people and wildlife.

Critics have described the process of rewilding as having all the hallmarks of the movie *Jurassic Park*, with concerns ranging from the re-introduction of predator mega-species (i.e. wolves in Yellowstone Park), to the unknown knock-on effects of re-introducing plant or animal species into ecosystems that have been modified through human intervention such as urbanization. Genetic re-engineering designed to bring back species from the brink has also been a contro-versial experiment within the rewilding movement.

Celebrity proponents such as writer George Monbiot argue that rewilding is not about seeking to restore nature to a prior natural state, but rather to reintroduce missing nature into abandoned and degraded urban land. This is about 'resisting the urge to control nature and allowing it to find its own way'[16] and 'restore to the great-est extent possible ecology's dynamic interactions'.[17] Similarly, Rewil-ding Europe makes a distinction between restoration and rewilding. 'Rewilding is really not about going back in time. It is instead about giving more room to wild, spontaneous nature to develop, in a modern society.'[18]

The language of rewilding cities seems simple enough – to make cities wild again. But this simple statement raises many questions.

> What does it mean to be *wilder?* Wilder than what? What does it mean to be more *natural?* I am interested in *what* and, by exten-sion, *when* and *where* rewilding refers to as it has moved into various geographies across the globe.[19]

To really shift the language of cities to include 'wild', we must ask more fundamental questions that probe more deeply the actions and intentions of humanity, namely: 'why as a species do we behave in such a destructive way in the first place?'[20]

Castell's wild city

In 1977, the urban sociologist Manuel Castells wrote an essay, a provocation in which he focused on 'the urban question' as the lens for the capacity for humans to act destructively in cities. He wanted to take us beyond what he describes as the *myth of the urban crisis* to draw critical attention to the production of urban space within the conditions of late capitalism. Crisis is not, in this sense, an innately urban condition, but rather an ideological expression of the efforts of the political elite to naturalize societal tensions and contradictions. For Castells, what could emerge if civic and environmental movements fail in their resistance to market logic is a new and more sinister urban form: the wild city.

The failure of urban policies to handle problems generated by uneven development can lead to the breakdown of social order and development of protest organizations. As Castells notes, local governments and the provision of needs are separate and unequal, which prevents fair redistribution of urban infrastructure and services through the delivery of public goods. Challenges from the grassroots against structural logic may result in riots and the breakdown of social order as the physical manifestation of contradictory and uneven urban expansion and provision of services.

There is a normative edge here that reflects the ideals of the good city as a place of dignity, security, and harmony, where the greatest achievements of modern civilization should and could be available to all. In the United States, Castells argues the urban crisis was framed first around poverty and racial discrimination, and later as the key urban services, economic and fiscal crisis, and urban conflict. Conventional urban infrastructure problems such as unaffordable housing, poor transportation, pollution, and urban renewal, sit alongside broader community concerns around crime, violence, racial tension, and public immorality.

From Castell's Marxist perspective, urban crisis is a crisis of capitalist accumulation, urban structure and consumption, and reproduction of the ruling social order. The twin cleavers of economic dualism and spatial segregation reflect pockets of capitalist concentration driven by the political elite. Marxist economics would suggest that the central mechanisms within capitalism fail in two key ways: the provision of public infrastructure; and in the management of urban land-use development and outcomes.[21] Both of these failings in turn call for planning intervention, which often exacerbates the very issues it sets out to resolve.

For example, urban renewal and social programs, designed to improve the social and economic context, often work to accelerate and exacerbate social divisions and conflicts through population displacement and gentrification. As Marx highlights:

> Improvements of towns, accompanying the increase of wealth, by the demolition of badly built quarters, the erections of palaces for banks, warehouses etc. the widening of streets for business traffic, for the carriages of luxury, and for the introduction of tramways etc., drive away the poor into even worse and more crowded hiding places.[22]

Issues of land and property development, the relations between planning and markets, and the implementation impacts of planning instruments all take place within what urban geographer David Harvey describes as 'feral capitalism'.[23] Within feral capitalism, this process of understanding and translation leading to action is further complicated by predatory development funding practices and the associated vast terrain of land speculation and accumulation (often by dispossession) that impact on those most vulnerable. For Harvey there is an inevitable trajectory of creative destruction through urban growth and development that results in social and ecological destruction.

Feral capitalism has particular emphasis on speed, which pays due homage to the three 'Es' of economy, efficiency, and effectiveness. Land reform through planning is central to what urban geographers Scott Lash and John Urry describe as 'fast capitalism': the 'speeding up and stretching out' of the processes of production and consumption through the use of technology that forms part of the growth cycle of a hyper-competitive market.[24] This affects both the social and environmental realms, whereby 'the earth is being held by the muscular arms of the entrepreneur-plurocrats, like it, or not'.[25]

The focus on urban land supply at low cost for development amidst calls for greater economic competitiveness through reductions in planning controls have ignited public concern about the quality of space and place, liveability, equity, and environment. As Marx noted previously in the *Grundrisse*,

> The important thing is not the market's distance in space but the speed – the amount of time – by which it can be reached ... the

velocity of circulation the time by which it is accomplished is a determinate of how often capital can be realized in a given time.[26]

The wild capitalist economy, as many have observed, offers both mode of seeing and means of organizing cities, but has no ethical platform, singular logic, or essential form. Capitalism exists to a large extent parasitically, drawing momentum and sustenance from the earth and others as opportunity arises and provides. The promise, and indeed for those privileged within the system, the reality, is one of endless possibilities. Nowhere is this expressed more powerfully and viscerally than in the city. For David Harvey it is always the shifting logic of capitalism that plans the role of planning.

For Castells, the wild city is the expression of urban crisis in this system of production and distribution and the failure of trickle-down economic theory in response to inadequate provision of housing, transportation, health, and education as key examples – and more recently greenhouse gas emissions and climate change.

Urban activist movements are predominantly a community response to these issues. The larger the response, the greater the crisis, both of formal politics but also fundamentally in the mechanisms of urban production, consumption, and (re)-distribution. As Castells notes, the response from the elites can be harsh and swift, and the role of planning in this process can often be benign or at worst complicit as co-conspirators with the political urban elite.

> The Establishment is violent in development of repressive apparatus top-bottom social order, urban movements are repressed and discouraged and meanwhile the urban planners attend more international conferences in the outer, safer world.[27]

Wild country

'Toward what kind of futures are we being led by savage, fanatical capitalism?'[28] For Quandamooka artist Megan Cope, 'Colonisation is the monster, it's a machine, it's a process, it's a project turning everything that is sacred and sentient into death and trauma.'[29] An important corollary to Western capitalism, but in many senses a significant precursor to it, is the role of settler societies and the violent brutality of colonization and Indigenous land dispossession. The 'we' in this sense are the settler-colonizers and 'white-fella' conquerors and their mostly city-dwelling descendants.

Cities are intimately connected with the organization of human life, and the urban way of life is the preeminent condition for populations across the globe. However, as cities dominate over their hinterlands through structurally regressive mechanisms of redistribution, so too do different parts of the city dominate others legitimized through contested land claims and political struggles. The problem is that we live in a society where wild settler capitalism and postcolonialism have run amok amidst 'the animal instincts of the entrepreneur'.[30]

At the heart of these urban planning and sustainability tensions within cities is the land question. The processes of land and property development are central to urbanization and the production of space, community, and place. Within an urban context, this includes the goods, infrastructure, human labour, and market use value and exchange this type of land embodies. 'The role of landownership, the organization of the construction industry and the nature of funding mechanisms and acting intermediaries such as developers and planning consultants are critical to understanding urban development processes.'[31]

If the land question is at the broken core of contemporary wild capitalism, then it is made manifest in cities through the dynamics of the housing market, property ownership, and development infrastructure. These processes reflect the power relations between state and market, the nature and role of the planning system, as well as shifting community perceptions, spatial dynamics, and place qualities. For Castells, 'Urban society is never merely spatial form but urban culture – values, norms, and social relations – that possess a historical specificity and logic of organization and transformation.'[32]

It is no coincidence that the Ancestral Remains of Indigenous peoples from around the world were stolen and illegally exported until the 1940s. Their removal and instalment in museums, and relocation in museums as objects of scientific study and public curiosity, occurred as part of the wider colonial project. To have the remains returned home for a proper, respectful burial has been the focus of first nation campaigns over the last 50 years – with mixed success. In Australia, it is estimated that up to 10,000 Aboriginal and Torres Strait Islander people remain in the nation's museums, despite repeated pleas for them to be returned.

Museums Victoria has acknowledged publicly that it has been 'part of a really sad history' with the indignity and harm suffered then by Aboriginal and Torres Strait Islander people, still experienced to this day. Museums Victoria's current strategic plan focuses on placing 'living cultures, histories and knowledge at the core of Museums Victoria's practice' in partnership with First Peoples.

During the nineteenth century, museums across the globe actively collected human remains to study and display the bodies of Indigenous peoples. These remains were mostly acquired without the permission of Indigenous peoples; bodies were stolen from graves, causing great and continuing distress to people and communities. This difficult and painful history has resulted in many First Peoples individuals and communities experiencing great distress and sadness from the display of human remains – whatever country or people they belong to – should be laid to rest and not on display.[33]

'Wild people (colonizers) make Wild country (degrading and failing).' This is how anthropologist Deborah Bird Rose describes the context for decolonization in *Reports from a Wild Country*. The violent concept of 'the wild' pervades the book, which explores the possibilities for reconciliation between Indigenous and 'settler' people and nature, within the context of both genocide and ecocide. Settler societies are built, she argues, on a dual war: 'a war against nature and a war against the natives, and each has been devastating'.[34]

Rose highlights the irony and paradoxical nature of the concept of wild in this context as evidenced in the description of the invader Captain Cook by Hobbles Danayarri, who is a now deceased Indigenous Yarralin lawman and community leader. 'As Hobbles liked to say, Captain Cook was the real wild one. He failed to recognize the Law, destroyed people and country, lived by damage, and promoted cruelty.'[35] In the same context, she offers up a situated understanding of wild country based on her discussion with Indigenous elders. 'Quiet country stands in contrast to the wild: man-made and cattle-made.'[36]

The social and ecological impacts of this damage is about multi-generational catastrophe and violence, death and devastation. Rose argues this goes to the core of the problem for settler societies. The hope of new worlds and better societies – the quest for the good city – is built on the destruction and erasure of Indigenous ways of life and ecosystems. We glamorize the frontier of civilization, fetishize the violence of colonization, and erect walls of silence that keep us blind to the ongoing livingness of Country.

> The attempt to transform the wild places and the wild person into civilized place and civilized person was an attempt to fill an emptiness with culture: it resulted in the creation of emptiness.[37]

We mostly live in cities, but we are situated in damaged and wounded Country. Founded in this disjuncture and detached from our moral accountability, how, Rose asks, can we (the wild) possibly process or progress a politics of decolonization or 'de-wilding'? The path towards reconciliation depends on recognizing the connection between Indigenous and settler people and place, leading to an ethical commitment of intention, and not just relying on hope to usher in a different kind of future.

Meanwhile, we retreat to our wildly unsustainable cities: wasteful of water, food, and energy, and ignorant to the spiritual and cultural connection of Indigenous people to their land. The effects of our 'she'll be right' attitude are felt not just locally, but globally.

> Australia is very much part of the global scene, both in the number of extinctions and in the production of the waste and damage (including greenhouse gases) that promotes extinctions. The violence wrought on indigenous ecosystems, the practice and making of the 'wild', is both long-standing and ongoing ... in the wake of settler ecocide, Australian settlers, by our own actions, can only inhabit what is for us 'wounded space'.[38]

For Rose, alternatives to the 'wild' can be found in the past and in the present and can arise unexpectedly, from both people and place. 'Alternatives are entangled in the midst of the wild, and depend on the wild, even as they resist it ... entanglement give us grounds for action.'[39]

Urban wildness

The lyrical children's fable *Where the Wild Things Are*[40] by American writer and illustrator Maurice Sendak tells the story of Max, a young boy who likes to dress up in a wolf suit and cause havoc in his home. The title of the book is based on the Yiddish expression *vilde chaya* (wild animals).[41] In the story, Max's bedroom transforms into a jungle island inhabited by strange and mythical beasts known as the Wild Things.

Time magazine wrote that what makes this best-selling children's book so compelling is its grounding effect that seeks to balance the seesaw of human fear and comfort. The message from the author is that 'there's a Wild Thing in all of us and that's okay, it's what makes you human'.[42] 'And the walls became the world all around.' At home, Max has a tantrum and is sent to his room without any supper. 'He travels to a far-away land, which is inhabited by the Wild Things. Max proves himself to the Wild Things by partaking in a wild rumpus so they make him their King. But he is homesick and craves his own room and home. But the Wild Things do not want him to go and cry, '*Oh please don't go – We'll eat you up – we love you so!*'[43] Max returns to his bedroom to find a hot supper waiting for him.

On many levels, this story could be read as the settler-colonial fantasy of mastery and separation from nature/other: the petulance and discontent with society; the quest for adventure and flight of fancy to new lands; the domination of the Indigenous population; the sense of alienation and nostalgia for home; and finally the mistaken belief in the inherent good of conquest and colonization.

Where is the wild in the city? There is no easy answer to this deceptively simple question. For we are the wild in the city, as much as we are the destroyer of the wild. Building on sociologist Bruno Latour's idea of 'wild things', the city as an assemblage of all manner of things and practices needs 'a politics of the wild without recourse to old binaries of nature and society', us and them, good and wild. How do we imagine ourselves to be civilized? How is exclusion performed? How is our concept of civilization grounded in that exclusion?[44] If we accept that we are in the midst of systemic ecocide, what can we do to shift that?

Cities are very much a human-centred story and more specifically in the West, a settler-colonial-centred story. The *dispotif* or the institutional, physical and political mechanisms and knowledge structures that maintain this power, suggests geographer Susan Ruddick, is what anchors the 'western civilized man'. The division of the civilized human and 'other' is not the *effect* of the civilizing act, but rather its very *foundation*, underpinning everything that it means to be civilized.[45] To address this will require a more thoroughly problematic glimpse of our habits and hubris – our estrangement and alienation in the past and present – in order to discover and engage with the *urban nature* of our wild cities and ourselves as we move into the uncertain future.

Ruddick's interest is not just in the entrenched existence of the divide between human and non-humans in urban spaces and places, but the work this divide does to create a particular kind of imaginary of what the urban is, could or should be. For Ruddick, this approach renders the urban simultaneously 'placeless and pervasive' on a planetary scale, structured with a logic that asserts the urban is code for 'a way of life under capitalism'.[46] Urban galaxies and the perforation of traditional divides are now at a more than planetary scale. The urban emerges as a chaotic construction, shape shifting and unpredictable in form and content, and like the wild, found everywhere and nowhere.

Urban development works, including the clearing of natural vegetation, for example, have recently resumed on widening the Western Highway near the Australian regional city of Ararat in the state of Victoria. The highway serves as a major freight line for trucks delivering food and goods across the state border between the capital cities of Melbourne in Victoria and Adelaide in South Australia. The widening and development of the dual highway will destroy thousands of native trees, including around 250 sacred trees, some up to 800 years old.

These trees are a living heritage of deep cultural significance and practice for the local Djab Wurrung traditional owners who are fighting this decision. They reject the rationale that supports the widening of a highway over the preservation of significant living cultural heritage and ask for its protection. 'We ask that this impending destruction as part of VicRoads works be halted immediately, more appropriate respect for the concerns of the Djab Wuurung community be taken into consideration, and that the trees and the site are protected.'[47]

In Australia, the law protects trees if they are considered threatened, endangered, or vulnerable. Indigenous plant species, for example, may be protected under the *Environment Protection and Biodiversity Conservation Act 1999*. Vegetation may be protected more broadly as part of the public estate (such as in national parks, for instance). Native vegetation on private land may also be protected to conserve biodiversity and preserve habitat for endangered species.

Recognition of the role of traditional owners, which includes protection of Country, is a contested issue in Australia. Federal and state government laws may protect 'significant' trees through heritage and/or Aboriginal heritage legislation. Or they may not. The Djab Wurrung have challenged both state and federal government decisions against heritage protection for the sacred trees and their surrounds. Activists have set up camp to protest the destruction of the trees – grandmother birthing trees, their companion grandfather trees, and direction trees.

> [Settlers] can't understand what it means to be able to connect the blood coursing through your body to ancestors' blood soaked in ancient soil and ancient trees. To sit in a tree that saw your people birthed, your people massacred, and now your people's resistance is a feeling that the English language will never be able to capture … This connection may be … poetic but this connection is a threat. It is a feeling that reinforces our rights to this land. This

connection must therefore, by the logic of the settler state, be destroyed.[48]

In New Zealand, the Whanganui River, which flows 145 kilometres to the sea in the central North Island, now has legal standing. The law recognizes the Maori Iwi people's sacred relationship with land and water. Through this legislation, the Whanganui River is recognized as a person when it comes to the law. According to the Minister for Treaty of Waitangi negotiations, the river has

> its own legal identity with all the corresponding rights, duties and liabilities of a legal person ... this legislation recognises the deep spiritual connection between the Whanganui Iwi and its ancestral river and creates a strong platform for the future of Whanganui River.[49]

Communities are starting to advocate for the rights of nature to exist, thrive, and evolve. Similar 'rights of nature' laws, which change the legal status of nature, exist in Ecuador, Bolivia, Colombia, India, and Uganda, to name a few. Under the Yarra River (Wilip-gin Birrarung murron) Act 2017, while the river's legal status has not changed, there is progressive recognition of the connection between the traditional owners and the river. As the preamble to the act states, 'This Act recognises the intrinsic connection of the traditional owners to the Yarra River and its Country and further recognises them as the custodians of the land and waterway which they call Birrarung.'[50]

The Wild Law and associated Earth Jurisprudence movements present a vision of transforming the systems that structure and order industrialized societies to enable a role for letting all species flourish within the Earth community. This is described as an 'Earth-centred approach to ordering human societies, how to apply it, and its emerging role as a common manifesto for promoting social and environmental justice, the conservation of biological and cultural diversity, animal rights and welfare, and green spirituality'.[51]

The premise is that our legal system is a reflection of the values of those who make and administer the law, and this needs to be changed to address the damage and devastation that has been caused in the name of progress. This includes addressing the erasure of Indigenous people's rights and experiences, which often underpins calls for a return to 'pristine' nature in cities.

We need far better legal recognition of the role of traditional owners, which includes cultural and environmental heritage protection. Indigenous perspectives, developed on Country in holistic ways incorporating lore/law, have a particularly valuable contribution to make to address the settler-colonial legacy and capitalist DAMAGE: that is 'Dualism (of humans and nature), Anthropocentricism, Materialism, Atomism, Greed (individualism gone mad) and Economism (the myth of no boundaries and limitless opportunities)'.[52]

In the current political environment, deeply locked into a culture and mindset of economic growth and property ownership, 'you'd have to be dreaming'.[53]

It is no surprise that the urban wilds are weakly imagined in urban civilization futures, if considered at all. Thoreau's famous dictum 'in wildness is the preservation of the world' referred not to wilderness but instead to a state of humanity. Nature, like the wild, is not 'out there' separate from cities, but instead deeply integrated into our cities and lives as part of everyday situatedness, living and interaction. This is a continuum that positions separateness and alienation *from* nature/ each other at one dystopian end of the cityscape spectrum, versus connectivity and entanglement *with* nature/each other at the other as a pathway for shared urban and earthly futures.

How can we tell the story of cities in ways that shape our urban encounters differently? In *Being Salmon, Being Human – Encountering the Wild in Us and Us in the Wild*, Martin Mueller focuses on how our urban lives are mirrored in the lived experience of others around us – human or non-human – and how alternatives might be forged in the encounter and entanglements between us. 'To seek tracks out of the story of human exceptionalism is not to "leave story" entirely. It is rather to look for what other stories struggle to be born from the compost of the old.'[54]

As Tony Birch describes of growing up in Melbourne, and sharing this experience with his students in the context of climate change:

> I talked about *country* in the sense that Indigenous communities in Australia understand and experience it. We talked about a future, shared or not shared – the latter of which leads to our further disconnection from each other and place. Finally, I asked each student a question: 'What are we seeking when we speak of climate justice?' The universal response was not restricted to justice for humans alone. My students had come to believe that if we fail to care for country, it cannot care for us.[55]

If we are the wild city, then care for each other and Country is the key.

Notes

1 Attenborough, D (2016) 'Planet Earth II', BBC, accessed on www.bbc. co.uk/programmes/p02544td

2 Holvey, C (2016) 'Why Wild Cities are Good for our Health', BBC Earth, 9 December, accessed on www.bbc.com/earth/story/20161208-why-wild-cities-are-good-for-our-health

3 Wild Cities (2020) accessed on https://wildcities.org/our-purpose/vision-and-mission/

4 Ibid.

5 Avon Wildlife Trust (2020) 'My Wild City', accessed on www.avonwild lifetrust.org.uk/mywildcity

6 Remember the Wild (2020) 'Connecting People with the Natural World', accessed on www.rememberthewild.org.au/

7 Ibid.

8 Remember the Wild (2020) 'About Us – Connecting With our Environment', www.rememberthewild.org.au/about-us/

9 Thompson, H (1971) *Fear and Loathing in Las Vegas*, Penguin, London.

10 Kahn, P and Hasbach, P (eds) (2013) *The Rediscovery of the Wild*, MIT Press, Cambridge, MA, p. i.

11 Evernden, N (1992) *The Social Creation of Nature*, Johns Hopkins University Press, Baltimore.

12 Evernden, N (1993) *The Natural Alien: Humankind and Environment*. University of Toronto Press, Toronto.

13 Hinchcliffe, S, Kearnes, M, Degen, M, and Whatmore, S (2005) Urban Wild Things: A Cosmopolitical Experiment, *Environment and Planning D: Society and Space* 23: 644.

14 Ibid., p. 645.

15 Pettorelli, N, Durant, S, and du Toit, J (2019) *Rewilding*, Cambridge University Press, Cambridge.

16 Monbiot, G (2013) *Feral: Searching for Enchantment on the Frontiers of Rewilding*, Penguin, London, p. 9.

17 Ibid., p. 83.

18 Rewilding Europe (2020) 'Frequently Asked Questions', accessed on https://rewildingeurope.com/frequently-asked-questions-2/

19 Jorgensen, D (2015) 'Rethinking Rewilding', *Geoforum*, 65: 482.

20 Ibid., p. xvi.

21 Dear, M and Scott, A (1981) *Urbanization and Urban Planning in Capitalist Society*, Methuen, New York.

22 Marx, K (1867) *Capital. A Critique of Political Economy*, Progress Publishers, Moscow, p. 812.

23 Harvey, D (2012) *Rebel Cities: From the Right to the City to the Urban Revolution*, Verso, London, p. 157.

24 Lash, S. and Urry, J. (1994) *Economies of Signs and Space*, Sage Publications, London.

25 Citigroup Research (2006) *Revisiting Plutonomy: The Rich Getting Richer*, 5 March, p. 3.

26 Marx, K. (1973) *Grundisse*, London: Penguin, p. 538.

27 Castells, M (1979) 'The Wild City', in Feagin, J (ed.) *The Urban Scene – Myths and Realities*, Random House, New York, p. 68.

28 Davis, M and Monk, D (2007) *Evil Paradises: Dream Worlds of Neo-liberalism*, The New Press, London, p. ix.

29 Cope, M cited in Dow, S (2020) 'Meth Kelly and Colonial Monsters: Australia's Biggest Art Shows get Indigenous Rewrite', *The Guardian*, 25 February, accessed on www.theguardian.com/artanddesign/2020/feb/25/meth-kelly-and-colonial-monsters-australias-biggest-art-shows-get-indigenous-rewrite

30 Harvey, D (2012) *Rebel Cities: From the Right to the City to the Urban Revolution*, Verso, London, p. 157.

31 Healey, P and Barrett, SM (1990) 'Structure and Agency in Land and Property Development Processes', *Urban Studies*, 27(1): 89–104.

32 Castells, M (1975) 'The Wild City: An Interpretation of Research and Analysis on the US Urban Crisis', *Kapitalstate*, 4–5: 1–30.

33 Museum Victoria (2020) 'Aboriginal Human Remains and Museums in Australia', accessed on https://museumsvictoria.com.au/article/museums-victorias-position-on-displaying-human-remains/

34 Rose, DB (2004) *Reports From a Wild Country: Ethics for Decolonisation*, Griffin Press, Sydney, p. 34.

35 Rose, DB (1984) 'The Saga of Captain Cook: Morality in Aboriginal and European Law', *Australian Aboriginal Studies*, 2: 24–39; Rose, DB (2001) 'The Saga of Captain Cook: Remembrance and Morality', in Atwood, B and Magowan, F (eds), *Telling Stories: Indigenous History and Memory in Australia and New Zealand*, Allen and Unwin, Sydney, pp. 61–79.

36 Rose, DB (2004) *Reports From a Wild Country: Ethics for Decolonisation*, Griffin Press, Sydney, p. 4.

37 Ibid., p. 145.

38 Ibid., p. 36.

39 Ibid., p. 6.

40 Sendak, M (1964) *Where the Wild Things Are*, Red Fox, London.

41 Shea, Christopher (2009) 'The Jewish Lineage of "Where the Wild Things Are"', *The Boston Globe*, 16 October, accessed on http://archive.boston.com/bostonglobe/ideas/brainiac/2009/10/the_jewish_line.html

42 Pols, M (2009) 'Where the Wild Things Are with Sensitivity', *Time Magazine*, 14 October.

43 Sendak, M (1964) *Where the Wild Things Are*, Red Fox, London.

44 Hinchcliffe, S, Kearnes, M, Degen, M, and Whatmore, S (2005) 'Urban Wild Things: A Cosmopolitical Experiment', *Environment and Planning D: Society and Space*, 23: 643.

45 Ruddick, S (2015) 'Situating the Anthropocene: planetary urbanization and the anthropological machine', *Urban Geography*, 36(8): 1113–30.

46 Ibid., p. 1114.

47 Change.org (2020) 'Protect Sacred Djab Wurrung Birthing Trees from Expansion of the Western Highway by Vicroads', accessed on www.change.org/p/daniel-andrews-protect-sacred-djapwurrung-birthing-trees-from-expansion-of-the-western-hwy-by-vicroads

48 Gorrie, N (2019) 'The Government Wants to Bulldoze My Inheritance: 800 Year Old Trees', *The Guardian Australia*, 12 April, accessed on www.theguardian.com/commentisfree/2019/apr/12/the-government-wants-to-bulldoze-my-inheritance-800-year-old-sacred-trees

49 Roy, E (2017) 'New Zealand River Granted Same Rights as Human Beings', *The Guardian*, 16 March, accessed on www.theguardian.com/world/2017/mar/16/new-zealand-river-granted-same-legal-rights-as-human-being

50 Yarra River (Wilip-gin Birrarung murron) Act, accessed on www.legislation.vic.gov.au/in-force/acts/yarra-river-protection-wilip-gin-birrarung-murron-act-2017/004

51 Cullinan, C (2002) *Wild Law: A Manifesto for Earth*, Green Books, Cambridge.

52 Bosselman, F, Eisen, J, Rossi, J, Spence, D, and Weaver J (2010) 'Energy, Economics and the Environment: Cases and Materials', in Maloney, M and Burden, P (eds), (2014) *Wild Law: In Practice*, Routledge, Abingdon.

53 *The Castle* (1997) Australian movie, accessed on www.imdb.com/title/tt0118826/

54 Mueller, M (2017) *Being Salmon, Being Human: Encountering the Wild in Us and Us in the Wild*, Chelsea Green Publishing, Chelsea, VT, p. xvii.

55 Birch, T (2018) 'Recovering a Narrative of Place', *Griffith Review, First Things First*, 60: 1, accessed on www.griffithreview.com/articles/recovering-narrative-place-stories-climate-change-tony-birch/

6   Planning *in* climate change

The need for speed

The need for speed grips the contemporary imagination. Run. Fast. Change. Act. Go. Now! Urgent action is needed to address the climate emergency to bring greenhouse gas emissions down to the 1.5°C target or lower to prevent global warming, which will make the planet uninhabitable and result in species extinction. The *coronavirus* COVID-19 demands a fast response for public health restrictions and responsibilities to flatten the pandemic curve and save lives. Addressing catastrophic weather events such as bushfires and floods requires rapid, immediate action to halt or reduce the threat and restart the recovery.

These crises all sit alongside – many argue 'inside' – a dominant political economy where 'time is money' and increased market growth and efficiency is the market of progress. Acceleration of the economy rather than deceleration is the driving leitmotif of twenty-first-century Western modernity. On the one hand, the rate and scale of urban change is for many like 'a windy day that never ends'.[1] On the other hand, the frustratingly slow transition to low-carbon cities and reduced emissions in the face of climate change creates its own tensions.

The message is perversely mixed. People are confused and discombobulated. Communities are confronted by the 'aimless trajectory of fast capitalism and the (possibly disastrous) failure of governments locked into high-growth economic policies to confront environmental threats'.[2]

For some, the future is where

> the rich will simply hide out in their castles desperately trying to consume all the good things in their lifetime ... that ruse of reason by which the neoliberal order both acknowledges and dismisses

the fact that the current trajectory of human existence is unsustainable.[3]

Planning with all its ambitions and aspirations for future thinking and action, embodies this paralysis and reflects these critical contradictions and tensions. Caught between regulatory bureaucracy and market-led development pressures, the task for planning requires nothing less than a complete reinvention of ambition. But 'what is to be done and who the hell is going to do it?'[4] The result has been paralysis – stasis.

Reflections in the urban planning literature emphasize the role of planning as intimately linked with the discourses of sustainability and the 'challenges of co-existence in shared spaces'.[5] Central to this endeavour are deeply existential questions that go to the core of professional identity and purpose: 'who are the planners?' and 'what do planners do?' This in turn has led to more critical questions related to 'planning for what and whom?' and how planning education and practice might be better focused to achieve progressive democratic, environmental and economic aims.

How does planning engage the community in co-designing, developing, and delivering strategic action in a climate of growth-led change? Who is the community that planning seeks to serve? Is it local, national, global, political, or virtual? By what democratic means and processes? What are the viable alternatives for planning – both sensitive and responsive – to the interdependencies and complexities of supporting and promoting sustainability?

Some argue that a planning system informed by a clear idea of the dynamics of markets 'is more likely to be in a position to strike good bargains for the community and the environment'.[6] As planning theorist John Friedmann observes, in a globalized world 'speed, movement, and power have been valued more than the fragile social infrastructure of place-based community'. In particular, he criticizes the lack of any plausible models for local-based transformative change and the need to offset speed with 'balance, effort, measure, frugality and proportion' as crucial underpinnings for urban governance *modus operandi* at all scales.[7]

'More haste less speed' is fast becoming the contemporary catch cry. Planning must address the unequal and asymmetric nature of climate change, where impacts are both local and global in scale, and affect multiple generations in ways as yet unforeseen. This is an unprecedented challenge and existential crisis for planning because the past and present cannot guide our actions into the future, although we can seek to better learn from our mistakes.[8]

Others seek a more radical planning pathway premised on alternative ways of organizing the city in order to build a different kind of city with a different kind of urbanization. Urban geographer David Harvey, for example, argues that 'what matters is not the particular mix of institutional urban arrangements, but rather the unified effect of collective political action'.[9] This is needed to address the excesses of capitalism and generate urban and environmental change.

This builds on the 'right to the city' as outlined by French philosopher and urbanist Henri Lefebvre, with a particular focus on lived experience of the city as a polity: 'the right to participate in urbanity, the right to appropriate the city not merely as an economic unit, but as a home and an expression of lived experience'.[10]

Planning must shift the task and ambition from simply being about 'building places' towards fostering the capacity for communities to understand and engage with how places and spaces are produced and change in order to generate the necessary transformation to sustainability. If the conditions of climate change operate in highly flexible and contingent ways, then there is pressure for planning to respond to the 'uncertainties arising from these multiple forces operating at multiple levels'[11] by developing a clear ethical focus to shape planning practice. This includes but is not limited to expanding the planning knowledge base available to our communities; enhancing democratic opportunity and debate; recognizing different forms of local knowledge, history, and politics; and co-developing community skills and practices.

> … perhaps the key message we can offer our polities at the present period is to encourage others to use the perceptions of instability and crisis in a strategic way, as an opportunity to take stock, to re-think policies, projects and practices, and to build the intelligence and coalitions which could bring future benefits for the many not just the few in our localities.[12]

Planning in a cul-de-sac

Debates about the relationship between planning theory and practice are well trodden paths. The nature and extent of the 'theory/practice divide' has filled numerous planning books and journals, most lately fomenting concern that planning is in a state of crisis with much of its theory having little to do with the work of most planners.[13] Counter arguments posit planning theory as the creative tension that defines and drives forward the field of practice by engendering both the reflective practitioner and the practical scholar.

Two key narratives are common. Narrative one is about the growing planning theory–practice divide, how distant and polarized these two endeavours have become, operating as if in two completely different worlds with little engagement or relevance to each other. Narrative two is linked to narrative one and seeks to bridge this divide by bringing these two parts closer together so that they become almost synonymous with each other, as if as one.

To understand the importance of these two narratives for the capacity for planning to respond to the contemporary context of climate change, requires delving back into the evolution of planning education, which sits at the nexus of theory and practice and has shaped and been itself shaped by this inherently relational planning agenda over time. Understanding this history has implications for where we are now, and how we might move into the future.

The history of modern planning is synonymous with the modernist project with antecedents in the Industrial Revolution. Modern Western planning emerged out of a focus on the condition of industrial cities and how best to improve this. The early planning practitioners were architects, engineers, social reformers etc., who wanted to create order, harmony, and a well-functioning city. They were driven by utopic visions of what the city could be and a focus on architectural design and engineering, social justice, strong economy, health and hygiene. The creation of zoning and separation of uses was ushered in for environmental and economic reasons, but also social reasons, which paved the way for class-based segregation.[14]

The potential of planning theory as a transdisciplinary endeavour to shape the planning field in practice and education has been defined as a triad of key tasks: 1) a *philosophical* task to guide planners in their work; 2) an *adaptive* task that highlights the constraints and opportunities for planning practice within the continually changing course of human affairs; and 3) a *translation* task, whereby concepts and knowledge from other disciplines are adapted and made accessible and useful for planning and its practices to support sustainability.[15]

Tertiary education around planning as separate from these other disciplines emerged in the United States and the United Kingdom in the 1920s, and much later in Australia in the 1950s, with lecturers from United Kingdom. Early planning education was studio and practice-based with a strong emphasis on practitioner mentoring and work placements. After World War II, this began to change as the number of planners needing to be educated increased and the academy itself grew and changed. University-educated planners started to go down two different paths. The majority still went into practice, usually with a state government department.

During this time, planning educators were less likely to be practitioners and did not need to have a background in practice, instead bringing in different sets of skills and knowledge including critical theory, politics and – to a lesser degree – economics. An increasing number of undergraduate planning students went on to do honours and then a PhD and entered academia to become the teachers of planning students, even if they had not ever practised as planners. To work in a university and teach planning required complying with academic requirements including validation with the academy in terms of appropriate qualifications and publications in reputable academic journals, few of which, if any, were planning focused.[16]

The style of education also shifted from studio- and practice-based approaches to a format of lectures and tutorials. Students with little practical knowledge would then go out into practice where they would learn on the job a different set of skills. Planning was booming, and whilst the division was noted, ambitions around the credibility of planning with university-based education (as opposed to a trade), aligned with a push for professional accreditation such as with architecture and engineering, kept the dissenters largely muted and at bay.

But by the 1970s and 1980s, planning in practice was also rapidly changing. The state and state-based planning was increasingly under attack by both left and right, who both wanted to see a smaller role for government, albeit for very different reasons. Planning was becoming increasing specialized around housing, transport, social and environmental design-based planning, as well as fragmented across the private and public sphere. At times, it simultaneously occupied both these spheres, as the state role became smaller and contracted out key planning roles to private consultants, including the drafting of policy and planning schemes, regulatory code approvals and strategic infrastructure planning design and provision, particularly around transport. Activist planners working for non-government organizations and not-for-profit groups protested against the planners working for multinational companies.

Planning in practice was unsettled, fractured and ideologically divided.

Academia mirrored this diversity and societal shifts, splintering across different ideological, political, and disciplinary lines. Just as there was no one unified planning practice, nor was there one unified planning academy, and no sense of a coherent body of theory. There were still jobs for planners, but the ambit of what was considered to be planning started to revolve predominantly around narrower visions of development and property decision-making processes.

This was a far cry from the ambitious city-wide planning of the Industrial Revolution, which had been widely critiqued for being state projects more dystopian than utopian in practice. Ironically, at the time the planning academy was expanding, the role of planning practitioners was diminishing – not in number, but in the nature of the work planners were now doing. Often the strongest critiques were led by planning academics, which further undermined the potential for progressive roles for planning practitioners.

Some planning practitioners looked across at academics during this time and complained of obtuse, unconnected, and disengaged theory emerging from academics that had never practised planning, and in many cases did not even focus on planning in their research. In some cases, they were right. Meanwhile, some academics looked across at planners and saw many 'oiling the wheels of capitalism' with little regard for people and place. In some cases, they were right.

The narrative became one of needing to 'bridge' the theory–practice divide, in particular to make theory practice-based, or at least more obviously relevant to practice. Initiatives were increasingly put in place such as the involvement of the Planning Institute in education and accreditation, and the return of studio-based planning and practice-based education, including a focus on work placements. Others actively resisted these initiatives, arguing universities were an opportunity to gain a perspective difficult to attain amidst the 'belly of the beast' in practice.

By the 1990s, planning was under threat in both the academy and in practice.[17] The neoliberal screws were tightening in both the academy (with funding cuts, casualization and job precarity, impact indicators, and research interference at the federal level) and in practice (with political interference and marginalization). Ironically, planners were blamed for the state of cities – a role from which they had long been marginalized by political and conservative interests. Academics began to be more vocal and come out as advocates in support of the planning project, using their research to push for changes in policy and legislation and defend planning.

Practitioners also started to realize that rather than 'closing the gap',[18] critical distance can be strategically useful. Academics could say things practitioners often could not in their roles, provide the empirical evidence base practitioners can draw on and, importantly, showcase, interpret, and translate much-needed new thinking and ideas for the climate of change. Academics for their part came to realize that some of the most innovative and exciting work was happening in real time in practice, and not 12 months later, when the journal article was published and read by other academics. Genuine impact and engagement are in critical praxis, where the fusion of ideas and practice lays the groundwork for transformative change.

But in all this, something important was lost. In seeking to bridge the divide, there was a push from both practitioners and many academics to rein in theory to focus on planning in practice. Just which theories are to be embraced and which are to be jettisoned is not clear. Is it sustainability, justice, equity, collaboration, economics, ethics, values? Theory is about ideas, concepts, and values, and always there in the lenses we use, the choices we make, the positions we defend – it is just not always made transparent.

Planning at the moment is almost a-theoretical with few new ideas/concepts/values (i.e. theory) being put forward, tested, critiqued, experimented with, debated, and discussed. This is not about research dissemination, and communication. This is about research impact and engagement with the ideas and practices that may re-shape, recast, or re-calibrate the way we see and do planning. The jettisoning of theory, particularly in Australian planning, has been an impoverishment for the planning and development of more sustainable cities and regions.

Not all planning practices are useful, successful, relevant – there is a lot of experimentation, which is at the heart of innovative practice. This does not mean that all practice is judged by one example or that all practice should fit a one-size-fits-all model and should be dismissed or taken away or made to conform. The same applies to planning theory. Not all theory is necessarily useful, successful, transferable, or even relevant.

Much theory, like practice, is a process of experimentation, testing exploring, engaging. Do these ideas work? Is this lens useful? Does this conceptual framework help re-orient the way we do things? This is an ongoing, restless quest – there is no end point, there is no one position. Innovation mobility travels different pathways. But, if you remove all the outliers, the experimental, the radical, then you are left with the status quo. And in our increasingly unequal and warming world, this is not enough anymore.

We face big planning challenges in this climate of growth-led change. We need creative and transformative planning ideas, concepts,

and theories to inform and be informed by creative and transformative planning practice. Those who specialize in planning theory
need to attend to that craft better. Like any craft, this means honing
skills and working harder to find and translate interesting planning
ideas, new lenses, creative ways of unsettling, or re-formulating areas
where we have become stuck.

This means better scholarship, which involves more reading and
less writing to achieve deep not shallow understandings, including
the historical antecedents of the work and previous critiques and
engagements; better translation to make complex ideas relevant and
understandable; and to be humble in offering these ideas in the face
of those who are in the frontline on a daily basis, and have incredibly valuable and interesting insights and stories to share. We all
gain from this.

We need to build up planning theory and practice in Australia and
elsewhere; it is currently in a very weakened and demoralized state,
right at the time we need it the most. The danger of this is that planning debates soon come to a cul-de-sac, focusing largely on the limited
sub-field of professional practice politics, which tends to 'quickly
change and become forgotten while the material legacy of planning
decisions remains for generations'.[19]

Planning and reform

The relationship between planning and reform has emerged as an increasingly double-edged sword that does not necessarily further progressive
democratic and environmental aims.[20] Progressive interests, especially
social movements and environmentalists, sought, from the 1970s,
changes to planning systems that were seen as sclerotic and insensitive to
ecological and human values. This advocacy helped build the case for
widespread reform, which in Australia during the 1980s and 1990s was
largely carried out during an era of wider neoliberal reform of the public
sector. Many environmental ambitions were denied as improved economic and administrative efficiency became dominant ambitions.

Within the Australian context, there have been a number of key
moments that have shaped and re-shaped the role of planning within
society more broadly. As indicated above, one strong agenda of
reform in Australia has been a platform for those who have sought a
more expansive interdisciplinary understanding of the political
domain of the broader planning project and its effect on Australian
society, economy, and environment. For example, during the 1970s, a
new social democratic reform context gained ascendancy with the

Whitlam Labor government, whose election promises included economic redistribution to those previously marginalized as well as
addressing the costs and disadvantages of growth.[21]

Planners during this era were urged to evolve as interdisciplinary
generalists with a largely socio-political and community-based
orientation.[22] However, by opening the space of political negotiation,
these progressive critiques unintentionally empowered those with
quite different – possibly contradictory – reform agendas such as the
proponents of a free-market society,[23] who prefer to see a reduced
role for the state.

The 1980s witnessed the rise of neoliberalism in Australia amidst
a substantive re-imaging of the national position, standing, and attitude relative to an increasingly competitive global world context.
Keynesian policy in post-war Australia was under siege amidst
increasing concerns around escalating foreign debt, poor trade performance, and the decline of manufacturing. The welfare mentality
of state paternalism, the so-called 'nanny state' that had guided Australia since the 1940s was in the process of being dismantled in order
to better facilitate innovative, entrepreneurial activity at the global
scale.

The federal Labor treasurer at the time, Paul Keating, famously
remarked that Australia would end up as 'a banana republic', 'a third
rate economy in an international hole' if it did not act swiftly to make
the 'adjustments' necessary to be competitive within a global
economy.[24]

What followed was a period of intense and rapid structural change
in terms of capital, labour, and the state. This was coupled with a re-
orientation of policy and institutional frameworks in order to open
the economy to global forces through a greater emphasis on market
orientation and a reduced role for the state. A 'new right' ideological
framework of faith in free-market capitalism rather than the state for
resource allocation and income distribution redefined Australia. This
spawned a raft of neoliberal policies designed to 'subordinate a wide
array of possible social goals to more narrowly defined economic priorities'.[25] At the urban scale, this agenda has subsequently emphasized
economic growth and competitiveness within the context of
globalization.

The new right political-economic reform agenda has significantly
re-shaped Australian planning in terms of its role, purpose, and
attendant spatially oriented policies, processes, practices, and roles.
Caught within the pervasive neoliberal reform agenda focused around
economic growth and investment, planners have struggled to find

ways to effectively respond to the pace of transformation within a market-oriented governance. Within this prevailing environment, Australian planning has been recast as a relatively narrow endeavour with planning tools 'so stripped of their effectiveness by notions such as "flexible planning" and discretionary decision-making, as to be almost the antithesis of the word planning'.[26]

Alongside the transformative agenda of neoliberal reform, a parallel reform movement around environmental sustainability has also been gaining force within Australia since the mid-1980s and early 1990s. As a meta-political discourse, environmental sustainability has penetrated at multi-scalar levels and raised important questions about the need for fundamental changes to the status quo in the face of the scope and seriousness of the environmental problems confronting humankind. Although largely separate from the debates around political reform and economic restructuring, the impact of this international agenda has been strongly felt in Australia, leading to increased political leverage to government policies and processes.

The imperative of environmental sustainability, and the need for new ways of imagining and balancing the sustainability tripartite of economic development, environmental concerns, and social justice, jostles for space on the national political platform. Central to the discourses surrounding environmental sustainability are the possibilities broadly outlined in the Brundtland Report (1987) of the need to meet the needs of the present without compromising the ability of future generations to meet their own needs.

The formal Australian response to this initially emerged through the 1992 National Strategy for Ecologically Sustainable Development (NSESD), which recommended an expanded conceptualization of the terms 'progress' and 'development' to look beyond economic considerations to include ecological dimensions and social improvements in areas such as justice, education, and community participation. The NSESD emphasized the need to consider, in an integrated way, the wider economic, social, and environmental implications of decisions and actions and the development of new processes to support long-term rather than short-term environmental objectives.

A quite different reform agenda has emerged in the shadows of climate change, recasting the spatial ambit of Australian planning in its wake. The 'de-greening of ESD policy' and the new primacy given to economic growth from the late 1990s have been linked with a series of conservative agendas in government.[27] The climate change imperative has further exposed the lack of recognition of the scale of the problem, urgency of the situation, and development of real strategic vision. This has been linked to a political culture 'obsessed with short-term economic priorities and ideologically committed to market-based approaches'.[28]

Despite declarations of a climate emergency, planning and reform around sustainability and climate change have been largely muted by the endless quest for greater economic growth and competitiveness, which have combined to recast Western planning since the 1980s as anti-planning or 'pseudo-planning'.[29] This is far removed from the social justice origins from which modernist planning began. There is growing recognition that the scope and scale of the climate change challenge demands quite different understandings of planning in both theory and practice than has ever occurred before. This 'diabolical'[30] urban planning and policy challenge demands a better understanding of both the drivers as well as possible responses to climate change in cities, which must include efforts towards both mitigation and adaptation.

Australian urban scholar and social justice advocate Patrick Troy argues that this constitutes a need to reframe what constitutes the 'good life'. The problem lies in the maldistribution of consumption that underpins urban inequity.

> Climate change goes to the heart of the sustainability and con-
> tinuity of our society ... We need not only explore the distribu-
> tional issues raised by the impact of climate change on the
> Australian population but also on other populations. We need to
> do this to clarify what we mean by 'progress' and how it is to be
> measured so that we may understand better the balance between
> 'progress' and 'planet'.[31]

To really address this means looking backwards to understand how urban growth and development in Australian cities has brought with it largely unrecognized costs; looking at the present to see how collective action is finding ways to work to navigate and mitigate the effects of anthropocentric climate change; and looking to a future where the nature and magnitude of climate change as a justice agenda is clearly reflected in the processes and practices of public policy and planning.

> For any optimism about our future, Australians must move
> beyond our rugged individualistic past to search for a collabora-
> tive, cooperative approach to the resolution of the challenges of
> climate change. We may be able to salvage enough from our way

of living and how we approach and value others to construct a new way of respecting and working with them, to avoid the tipping point in the world's ecosystem towards which we are rushing.[32]

Planning and climate change

In 2008, the Garnaut Climate Change Review, jointly commissioned by Australia's state and national governments to examine the impacts of climate change, cautioned that, 'on a balance of probabilities, the failure of our generation on climate change mitigation would lead to consequences that would haunt humanity until the end of time'.[33] This echoed the message of the United Kingdom's Stern Report, which concluded that 'it is still possible to avoid the worst impacts of climate change; but it requires strong and urgent collective action'.

The Stern Report went further to caution that to 'delay would be costly and dangerous'.[34] This was a clear 'call to arms' for reconceptualizing planning firmly within the conditions of climate change in ways that embrace both the urgency and uncertainty of the climate change agenda, but also pathways to meaningful action.

Despite a broad commitment to sustainability and growing recognition of the urgency of climate change, the focus of planning remains coupled to the discourses of neoliberalism and the dilemmas of professional practice. Within the current professional and reform agenda, it is increasingly unclear for whom and for what this planning expertise serves.

Unlike the early reformist agenda that emerged in direct response to the conditions of poverty and squalor ushered in by the Industrial Revolution, planning 'the good city and region within the constraints of a capitalist political economy and a democratic political system'[35] has struggled to provide a strong focus and platform for responding to the imperative of climate change.

> All this is bad enough, but the greatest stupidity is that we build buildings in which we attempt to deny the climate with little regard for the energy cost. It is true that we are concerned to improve the efficiency of air conditioning, but this is really only at the margin. The solution is to rearrange or re-organize our affairs so that we consume less energy and reduce pollution. This is, admittedly, no new insight: the environmentalist movement has been saying this for years. Unlike doctors treating many of the

illnesses we suffer we are not confined to treating the effects. In cities, we can actually treat the cause.[36]

Climate change demands we focus on the building of shared knowledge and action that leads to transformative change alongside the necessary planning reform and review processes. This requires both short- and long-term strategic action and democratic co-ordination to take human settlement systems in a new and different direction. In short, climate change requires a planning response rich in understandings of space and place. Planning for its part needs to orient its collective efforts towards something greater than the tensions within itself. Three frames around climate change concurrently co-exist within planning.

Planning about climate change

Within this first frame, climate change is understood at arms' length – something that is still 'out there' in the distant future. Climate change may well exist but has yet to really penetrate or impact on the core business of planning. Climate change is considered to be something peripheral and disconnected to the everyday practices of planning. Planning activity in relation to climate change is considered to be needed for the future, if at all. This is the realm that largely defers to the sceptics and naysayers for whom climate change is little more than a theoretical consideration and contestable agenda played out largely in the media.

Professor of Earth Science Mark Maslin has described the influence of the five corrupt pillars of climate denial. The first is *science denial*, which argues that climate change is a natural process that has always occurred, and that contrary to the Intergovernmental Panel on Climate Change report claims, the science on climate change is unsettled, reliant on models and evidence that are inaccurate, distorted, or misrepresented. The second pillar is *economic denial*, which posits that even if climate change is occurring, it is too expensive to address without destabilizing society.

The third area is *humanitarian denial*, which focuses on the potential benefits to be gained from a climate changed globe such as warmer weather and more productive farming lands in some areas. Another key pillar is *political denial*, highlighting the dangers of taking action if other countries are not, and the need to focus on local priority issues rather than global responsibilities. Finally, the *crisis denial* focuses on the need to maintain the status quo – or life as we know it – and not rush into changes such as a shift away from fossil fuels to renewables given uncertainty about the outcome.[37] This is a perverse misuse of the precautionary principle.

The pervasive impact of these pillars of denial is reflected in planning policy and curriculum, in which climate change is marginalized and largely incidental within both higher education and professional development forums. Mirroring this larger strategic level of planning, from the underside, is the massive endeavour that defines and consumes much of everyday planning: development assessment. In this 'workhouse' of planning life, the professional is very likely to encounter the term 'climate change', but as a motherhood statement rather than a key shift in the field of human and ecological possibility.

For many planners, personal concern about climate change, and the reflection of this in changes to everyday work, are still distant, parallel universes.

As Patrick Troy wrote extensively, the form and structure of our cities was only made possible by low-cost fossil fuels – first coal, then petroleum. The consequence, he argued, is that we have cities in which we expend massive amounts of energy to transport people horizontally and vertically, to accommodate them and to deny the climate. Yet there are other ways of arranging the distribution of people and their activities so as to require lower levels of energy consumption and produce less pollution – and we must find these and act on them.[38]

In his later writing on climate change, he highlighted the need to explore the distributional issues raised by the impact of climate change on the Australian population, but also the impact on other populations. He advocated for a thorough planning and policy response to climate change in Australia, including a radical reimagining of systems for our land, water, and mineral use, and of housing, transport, and communication systems.[39]

Planning for climate change

In the second frame, climate change is recognized as an agenda that requires some interventionist planning action in the short term, with the intention of more strategic intervention to come later in the future. Within planning, climate change is positioned as just one of a suite of other 'wicked' planning interests and agendas such as affordable housing or public transport. Planning activity in this frame operates mostly at the strategic policy level or project level with the aim of building community resilience and encouraging adaptation strategies. This is still largely planning 'business as usual', with little in the way of substantive shifts to practice or pedagogy.

This is reflected in the United Nations Sustainable Development Goals (SDGs), where climate action (SDG13) is one of the 17 goals for 'peace and prosperity for people and planet now and into the future'.[40] The directive is urgent action to combat climate change and its impacts that recognizes 'with rising greenhouse gas emissions, climate change is occurring at rates much faster than anticipated and its effects are clearly felt worldwide'. However, the targets are soft and fuzzy including strengthening resilience and adaptive capacity, integrating climate change measures into policy and planning, increasing education and awareness, and taking steps to raise capacity for climate change planning.

The United Nations recognizes that

> while there are positive steps in terms of the climate finance flows and the development of nationally determined contributions, far more ambitious plans and accelerated action are needed on mitigation and adaptation ... strengthened capacities need to be scaled up at a much faster rate, particularly for least developed countries and small island developing States.[41]

The SDGs are an opportunity to take seriously the sustainable development challenges we face. In Australia, we could use the SDGs as a two-fold opportunity to ask the hard questions about the sustainability of our development and collectively explore transformative pathways, particularly within our cities. The SDGs can be mobilized to help achieve sustainable development and action on climate change, but are still a peripheral agenda in practice.

Within planning education, climate change is still largely an elective curriculum subject, with links developing across other core courses. At a professional development level, the emphasis is on one-off seminars, workshops, and guest lectures, which are increasingly well attended. An example of this frame is evident in the report 'Shifting Towards Sustainability: Education for Climate Change Adaptation in the Built Environment Sector', which addressed the need to increase the ability of planners to adapt to changes associated with climate change. Adopted by the Planning Institute of Australia, the ambitions of this endeavour recommended a focus on 'the commencement of discussions about professional development for climate change adaptation in a range of forums' and for university educators 'to begin to include climate change adaptation case studies within existing curricula'.[42]

Climate change is increasingly visible in planning, and the policy has noticeably shifted to the language of 'climate emergency'. The Planning Institute of Australia policy, for example, accepts the scientific assessments of the Intergovernmental Panel on Climate Change that human activity is changing our global climate, that irreversible change is already locked in, that the planning profession must address the reality of a changing climate, and that 'the decisions we make now as planners in guiding urban and regional development extend far beyond current influences and shape the future environments in which communities will live'.[43]

Despite these good intentions, in practice the approach within planning is still tentative, propositional, and even conversational – seemingly unable or unwilling to compel the substantive professional or institutional change needed. Cities in Australia and elsewhere still look and feel the same. Planners and planning educators carry on with business as usual, as if the crisis is sometime in the future – yet to come. Climate change is certainly part of 'the mix' of everyday planning, culture, and considerations, but still remains outside the sphere of disruptive shifts to the cultural status quo that are needed for meaningful urban change.

Planning in climate change

Planning in climate change emphasizes the immediacy and lived dimensions of climate change now and into the future. This understanding of climate change is intimately linked with planning praxis in all its diversity. Planning in climate change draws attention to the need for a profound change in the way planning theory and practice are conceived and undertaken in order to address the crisis conditions of climate change operating at multiple urban scales.

The 2019/20 bushfires in Australia brought climate change into the everyday citizen experience and global consciousness. The sense of crisis and urgency pricked the collective community consciousness into greater awareness and this led to action in response to the bushfires. What we are still yet to see is concerted and co-ordinated action in response to the climate change crisis more broadly.

Climate change offers an unprecedented challenge that requires fundamentally different ways of understanding and doing planning. In the last 50 years, there have been many critical advances in under-standing both the limits and potentialities of the work undertaken by planners grounded in 'an ethics of service, of inclusion, of knowledge-ability and of dynamic reflexive critique'.[44] But much more must be done in the here and now.

Anthropologist Deborah Bird Rose describes engagement with the 'here and now' as an ethical encounter and entanglement. We cannot help knowing we are here through damage, dispossession and death. We must not turn away from this past which has caused so much pain and harm. But what alternatives exist for us moving forward, and what is being asked of us? Addressing this, she argues, requires a moral engagement of the past in the present. This is without retreating to the future in which 'current contradictions and suffering will all be left behind justified by references to the future'.

Future orientation, Rose argues, 'has been a major tool deflecting us from moral responsibility',[45] an escape from accountability and responsibility.

For Rose, the pathway towards reconciliation is an open journey – social, spatial and temporal – and still possible to re-shape relations between people, place and environments. Decolonization depends on moving beyond the illusions of a comfortable life to the process of being present (a witness) to the moral claim being offered, the response, the recognition of connection, and commitment in the here and now, not sometime in the future.

Similarly, climate change as a pathway towards human–nature reconciliation also invites us to be present and bear witness to the 'here and now'. This is to build the knowledge and action that can lead to transformative change, without turning away from the destruc-tion, or defaulting to the imaginary future where some of us can seek to be washed clean.

Is this the legacy of the wounded space of colonisation and devel-opment: that having come into the world as signs of our fore-bears' lives, we now remake ourselves, and all who are enmeshed in our damage, as trackless ghosts?[46]

Our beds are burning

The Midnight Oil song 'Beds are Burning' is one of Australia's best-known protest songs. The band had recently toured the outback Indigenous communities with the Warumpi Band and

Gondwanaland as part of the Blackfella-Whitefella tour. It was here that the band learnt about giving lands back to the Pintupi people, who were among the last people to come in from the Gibson Desert, having been forcibly removed and sent to the Papunya Settlement 240km north-west of Alice Springs in the Northern Territory in the 1950s and 1960s. The Pintupi people left and established a new community in Kintore, about 250km west of Papunya in the 1980s.

The song was released just prior to the 200-year celebration of the arrival of Captain Cook in Australia on 26 January.[47] The song was a powerful anthem written to drown out the Australia Day anthem we were scheduled to be singing and remind Australians that the celebrations were founded on pillage and genocide of Aboriginal people and Country.[48] As Midnight Oil's Rob Hirst explains,

> I thought we could write a song about an ancient Australian community pushing back against all the shocking things that had been visited upon them ever since Europeans had arrived in this country.[49]

The song encourages a social activism that seeks to rise up and overcome the circumstances that have caused damage and destroyed both lives and Country by bearing witness and engaging with the entanglements of the present, in order to build a shared future. The song was covered recently by folk singing duo Angus and Julia Stone in 'Down to Earth' – a bushfire and climate relief concert held in Melbourne in 2020. Julia introduced the cover as a relevant song for the times.

> It was written 33 years ago about indigenous land rights and unfortunately, the lyrics and the meaning of the song is very relevant today. So let's try and change that. It's a shame that it takes a catastrophe to bring us all together in this world.[50]

Notes

1 Gleeson, B (2006) *Australian Heartlands: Making Space for Hope in the Suburbs*, Allen and Unwin, Melbourne.
2 Tomlinson, J (2007) *The Culture of Speed: The Coming of Immediacy*, Sage Publications, London, p. 154.
3 Davis, M and Monk, D (2007) *Evil Paradises: Dreamworlds of Neoliberalism*, The New Press, New York.

4 Harvey, D and Wachsmuth, D (2012) 'What Is to Be Done? And Who the Hell is Going to Do It?' In Brenner, N, Marcuse, P, and Mayer, M (eds), *Cities for People, Not for Profit*, Routledge, London, p. 264.

5 Healey, P (2008) 'Editorial', *Planning Theory and Practice*, 9(4): 431.

6 Healey, P (1992) 'Development Plans and Markets', *Planning Practice and Research*, 7(2): 19.

7 Friedmann, J (2010) 'Place and Place-making in Cities: A Global Perspective', *Planning Theory and Practice*, 11(2): 147.

8 See work by Deborah Bird Rose (2004) and Hannah Arendt (1958) for writing on hope in dark times.

9 Harvey, D (2012) *Rebel Cities: From the Right to the City to the Urban Revolution*, Verso, London, p. 87.

10 Merrifield, A (2002) *Dialectical Urbanism*, Monthly Review Press, New York, p. 156.

11 Thornley, A and Ryadin, Y (eds) (2002) *Planning in a Global Era*, Ashgate, Aldershot, p. 9.

12 Healey, P (2010) 'Re-thinking the Relations Between Planning, State and Market in Unstable Times', in Paolo, P and Vitor, O (eds), *Planning in Times of Uncertainty*, FEUP Edições, Porto, p. 15.

13 Hall, P (2002) *Cities of Tomorrow: An Intellectual History of Urban Planning and Design in the Twentieth Century*, Blackwell, Malden.

14 Fishman, F (2003) 'Urban Utopias: Ebenezer Howard, Frank Lloyd Wright and Le Corbusier', in Campbell, S and Fanstein, S (eds), *Readings in Planning Theory*, Blackwell, Malden, pp. 21–61.

15 Friedmann, J (2008) 'The Uses of Planning Theory: A Bibliographic Essay', *Journal of Planning Education and Research*, 28(4): 255.

16 Beauregard, R (2003) 'Between Modernity and Postmodernity: The Ambiguous Position of US Planning', in Campbell, S, and Fanstein, S (eds), *Readings in Planning Theory*, Blackwell, Malden, pp. 108–25.

17 Gleeson, B and Low, N (2000) *Australian Urban Planning: New Challenges, New Agendas*, Allen & Unwin, St Leonards.

18 In the Australian context I use that phrase with the cynicism and sadness it deserves.

19 Yiftachel, O (2007) 'Re-engaging Planning Theory: Towards South-Eastern Perspectives', *Planning Theory*, 5(3): 213.

20 Yiftachel, O (1998) 'Planning and Social Control: Exploring the Dark Side', *Journal of Planning Literature*, 12(2): 395–406.

21 See Leonie Sandercock and Mike Berry (1983), and Margo Huxley (2000).

22 Stretton, H (1970) *Ideas for Australian Cities*, Georgian House, Melbourne.

23 See Moran, A (2006) *The Tragedy of Planning: Losing the Great Australian Dream*, Institute of Public Affairs, Melbourne.

24 Paul Keating (1986) cited in Kelly, P (1992) *The End of Certainty*, Allen & Unwin, Crows Nest, p. 196.

25 Stilwell, F (2000) 'Changing Track: A New Political Economic Direction for Australia', Pluto Press, Annandale, p. 14.

26 Stein, P (1998) '21st Century Challenges for Urban Planning: The Demise of Environmental Planning in New South Wales', in Gleeson, B and Hanley, P (eds), *Renewing Australian Planning? New Challenges, New Agendas*, Australia National University, Canberra, p. 72.

27 Gleeson, B and Low, N (2000) *Australian Urban Planning: New Challenges, New Agendas*, Allen & Unwin, St Leonards, p. 162.
28 Lowe, I. (2006) 'A Big Fix: Radical Solutions for Australia's Environmental Crisis', Schwartz Publishing, Melbourne, p. 58.
29 See Lovering, J (2009) 'Editorial: The recession and the End of Planning as We Have Known It', *International Planning Studies*, 14(1): 1–6.
30 Garnaut, R (2008) *The Garnaut Climate Change Review Final Report*, Cambridge University Press, Melbourne.
31 Troy, P (2014) 'Climate Change Response: Linking Action, Policy and Research', *The Economic and Labour Relations Review*, 25(4): 627.
32 Ibid., p. 619.
33 Garnaut, R (2008) *The Garnaut Climate Change Review Final Report*, Cambridge University Press, Melbourne, p. 29.
34 Stern, N (2007) 'The Economics of Climate Change: The Stern Review', Cambridge University Press, Cambridge, p. xxvii.
35 Campbell, S and Fanstein, S (eds) (2003) *Readings in Planning Theory*, Blackwell Publishing, Malden, p. 1.
36 Troy, P (1999) *Serving the City – The Crisis in Australian Urban Services*, Pluto Press, Sydney.
37 Maslin, M (2019) 'The Five Corrupt Pillars of Climate Denial', The Conversation, November 29, accessed on https://theconversation.com/the-five-corrupt-pillars-of-climate-change-denial-122893
38 Troy, P (1995) *Australian Cities, Issues, Strategies and Policies for Urban Australia*, Cambridge University Press, Cambridge.
39 Troy, P (1996) *The Perils of Urban Consolidation: A Discussion of Australian Housing and Urban Development Policy*, Federation Press, Sydney.
40 UN (2020) 'Sustainable Development Goals', accessed on https://sustainable development.un.org/sdgs
41 UN (2020) 'Sustainable Development Goal 13: Taking Urgent Action to Combat Climate Change and Its Impacts', accessed on https://sustainable development.un.org/sdg13
42 'Shifting Towards Sustainability: Education for Climate Change Adaptation in the Built Environment Sector', p. 3.
43 PIA (2015) 'Planning in a Changing Climate, Planning Institute of Australia Policy', August, accessed on www.planning.org.au/policy/climate-change-0510
44 Healey, P (2003) 'The Communicative Turn in Planning Theory and its Implications for Spatial Strategy Formation', in Campbell, S and Fanstein, S (eds), *Readings in Planning Theory*, Blackwell, Oxford, p. 253.
45 Rose, DB (2004) *Reports from a Wild Country: Ethics for Decolonization*, University of New South Wales Press, Sydney, p. 18.
46 Ibid., p. 178.
47 www.songfacts.com/facts/midnight-oil/beds-are-burning
48 Mueller, A (2014) 'Australian Anthems: Midnight Oil – Beds are Burning', *The Guardian*, 11 March, accessed on www.theguardian.com/music/australia-culture-blog/2014/mar/11/midnight-oil-beds-are-burning-australian-anthems
49 Hirst, R (2019) 'How I wrote "Beds are Burning"', *Songwriting Magazine*, 5 May, accessed on www.songwritingmagazine.co.uk/interviews/how-i-wrote-beds-are-burning-by-midnight-oils-rob-hirst

50 Stone, J (2020) in Ramali, S, 'Julia Stone Covers Midnight Oil's "Beds Are Burning" Live for the First Time at Down To Earth Bushfire Concert', NME, 28 February, accessed on www.nme.com/en_au/news/music/watch-julia-stone-midnight-oils-beds-are-burning-down-to-earth-bushfire-concert-2615245

Wild Possibilities (Photographer: Russell Blamey)

7 Can the wild city be tamed?

The nature of crisis

What the bushfire victims in Australia and around the world in the 2019/2020 catastrophe could never have guessed, is that they were soon to be engulfed by a global health pandemic of a scale and severity to humanity never before encountered in modern times. As I write this chapter, I am in lockdown in my home in self-isolation, alongside many others across the globe. Everything looks the same. But nothing is the same. There is an undercurrent of anxiety and tension that pervades this 'new normal' and no one knows when this will end, or where to go.

> You can't assume anymore that people are not capable of infecting you. In many cases they won't even know they're infected. [You] have to kind of assume the rest of the world is a coronavirus soup. If I don't want to end up swimming in that bowl, I need to find another place.[1]

Coronavirus (COVID-19) is threatening humans, with more than 3 billion people going into lockdown within three to four months of the virus first emerging in China, and soon spreading to other areas. In Australia, you must stay at least 1.5 metres away from other people and there must be a density of no more than one person per four square metres of floor space. All non-essential businesses and services have been closed as well as state and national borders. Travel has been restricted or halted, and temporary hospitals and morgues set up in convention centres. Millions have lost their jobs, with governments pumping trillions of dollars into economic, health and welfare stimulus packages. Healthcare workers and carers are on the frontline. So are the poor, the sick, the elderly, the homeless and the vulnerable, as it ever was.

According to the United Nations Secretary General António Guterres, coronavirus is a global pandemic that affects all of humanity, regardless of location. 'Global action and solidarity are crucial. Individual country responses are not going to be enough ... Humanity must fight back.'[2] The relative speed with which the world has responded has given rise to hopes that the same lessons will be applied to addressing global climate change including the need to take action sooner rather than delay action. The temporary reduction in emissions as a result of reduced air traffic and personal vehicle movement has also been heralded by climate activists as a bright light in the otherwise devastating virus pandemic cycle that should be continued post-crisis.

The dramatic improvement in water visibility in Venice canals and *inter alia* the return of the visibility of aquatic life, for example, is a direct result of the reduction of tourists and urbanized boat traffic on the waterways. Improved visibility is not the same as quality, as the city mayor is quick to point out,[3] the latter being a far more systemic urban and environmental issue than a reduction in disturbed sediment coming to the surface. But it is a start.

Not so promising is the disruption to renewable energy and emissions reductions policies, which have been put on hold. Nor the looming peak oil and peak gas crises, which are being reported further down in the media after the coronavirus-related stories. Both the coronavirus and climate change crises consolidate the power status quo. This is the pattern of what has been described as 'disaster capitalism' in which a crisis is identified; the need for extraordinary politics in response to the crisis declared; this then overrides democratic norms and subsequently ushers in the capacity for the government/market to operate in ways unseen before.

Author and social activist Naomi Klein uses the term 'shock doctrine', to describe 'the brutal tactic of using the public's disorientation following a collective shock – wars, coups, terrorist attacks, market crashes, or natural disasters – to push through radical pro-corporate measures, often called shock therapy'.[4]

Hurricane Katrina turned into a catastrophe in New Orleans because of a combination of extremely heavy weather – possibly linked to climate change – and weak and neglected public infrastructure. The so-called solutions proposed at the time were the very things that would inevitably exacerbate climate change and weaken public infrastructure even further ... 'free-market' travellers were determined, it seems, to do the very things that are guaranteed to lead to more Katrinas in the future.[5]

Our collective response to crisis, whether in relation to coronavirus or climate change, is to try to 'flatten the curve'. The emphasis here is on acting swiftly to de-escalate and diminish – if not completely resolve – the crisis. We try to subdue, restrain, curb, and suppress the symptoms and impacts of the crisis. Blindly, we seek to tame the crisis that is 'out there'. Adaptation writ large will only take us so far. We urgently need to address the crisis 'in here'.

A tamed city

Coronavirus has been described as anti-urban, its cascading impacts affecting not just the health and mortality of the physical body, but also the lived sense of urban community and human connectivity. This finds expression in the spaces and places, the nooks and cracks of everyday urban life. Some commentators are asking if cities, as the 'epi-centres of capital and creativity from which new ideas and opportunities arise', can even survive coronavirus. Social isolation causes dysfunction, whilst urban 'proximity breeds serendipity and strength'.[6]

> [Coronavirus] exploits our impulse to congregate. And our response so far – social distancing – not only runs up against our fundamental desires to interact, but also against the way we have built our cities and plazas, subways and skyscrapers. They are all designed to be occupied and animated collectively.[7]

The sanitized city is the hallmark of Western enlightenment and modernity. But in response to coronavirus in the twenty-first century, the quest for cleanliness, health, and hygiene includes self-isolation and social distancing, and this is a very new – some say unprecedented – agenda for cities and their citizens in the urban age. On multiple levels, this is redefining the very idea of cities as one moment in broader urban processes. If the global coronavirus lockdown continues or rises, and most interactions become virtual or online, then what, if any, are the limits of what we are now prepared to call 'The City'?

The effects of a global social recession are predicted to outstrip the damage of the economic recession where most of the stimulus packages are currently being directed. The extreme in negative effects of solitary confinement as a key feature of incarceration practices is highlighted in the 2011 'United Nations Special Rapporteur on Torture and Other Cruel, Inhuman or Degrading Treatment or Punishment'.

Psychosocial experiences associated with individual isolation include depression, anxiety, panic attacks, hallucinations, difficulties with thinking, memory and concentration, and paranoia that leads to mental and physical breakdown.[8]

In the *Dangers of a Tamed City*, economic geographer and planning professor Robert Kloosterman highlights the transition from the interstitial spaces and places of the urban fringe subcultures in Amsterdam to mainstream gentrification (read here cultural sanitization). This was a result of increased levels of citizen affluence that came with higher income and education levels, which cleaned up the hippies, drugs, sex stores, and homelessness issues the city was previously (in)famous for.

Urban doyenne Jane Jacobs describes this as 'the self-destruction of diversity', whereby the processes of homogenization privilege particular communities or activities over others. This type of homogenization, Kloosterman argues, not only affects the quality of life of citizens, but actively increases the vulnerability of the city to crisis because the culture and economy are too one-sided. 'One should keep in mind a fully-tamed city is not just boring – it also ends up being a stagnating city.'[9]

Planning theorist Leonie Sandercock takes a different approach with her framework for the city planner tamed within the forces shaping twenty-first-century cities and regions: the consolidation of global capitalism; the rise of technology; the age of migration; the age of postcolonialism and the rise of Indigenous people; and the rise of civil society in the form of new social movements. Cotemporary planning, she argues, 'must define its role and play it in a world where governments almost everywhere are in retreat, fiscally overburdened and outmanoeuvred by the transnational investors whom they court'.[10]

This includes more politicized practices for planners seeking to create change including mobilizing community, engaging in protests and strikes, professional advocacy and the proposing and drafting of new laws to address inequity. Key literacies required are in the key areas of technology, design, ecology, multiculturalism, and critical analysis, put purposefully to work for the future of both people and planet.

Planning should be an ethical inquiry, with a 'frame of mind more humble, open, and collaborative than that of the heroic modernist planner'.[11] The emphasis is on situated understandings of context, culture, history, politics, and power, and the need to be present and bear witness to the entangled nature of the damage that has been inflicted on vulnerable people and places. This process of recognition and shared responsibility guides the necessary action around how we might live well and sustainably on the earth together.

Rather than tame or domesticate 'the urban wild', an ethic of care has surfaced as a rallying point for collective action in the Anthropocene. Care offers a powerful disruption to the binaries that bind and blind us such as good/wild, human/non-human, us/them. Author Maria Puig de la Bellacasa argues that this is because care is omnipresent, and this is its great power: as a mediating and connecting force we all hold in common. 'Like a longing emanating from the troubles of neglect, it passes within, across and through things. Its lack undoes, allows unravelling. Care is a human trouble, but this does not make of care a human-only matter.'[12]

The institutionalization of 'care' has a dark history (e.g. mental institutions, orphanages, nursing homes) and for many, this is the antithesis of the type of ethic that is needed to effectively address the challenges of contemporary times. For Aboriginal and Torres Strait Islanders, many of the attempts at institutional care in Australia have been cruel, mean-spirited and misguided: a mirror and manifestation of settler-colonialism that continues to this day. But for feminist scholars Joan Tronto and Berenice Fisher, an ethic of care includes 'everything we do to maintain, continue and repair our world so that we can live in it as well as possible'.[13] An ethic of 'caring-with' is one of seeking and enacting communal solidarity and 'care-full' justice in our imperfect worlds.[14]

How might our cities be different if 'to care' for people, other species and places, rather than 'to tame' them lay at the heart of planning wild cities in climate change? This is how we build urban resilience that makes a difference locally and globally.

Urban resilience matters

As a Melbourne resident, local community member, and mother, I pay my respects to the Wurundjeri people of the Kulin Nation on whose unceded lands I live and work. As the daughter of Western, white privilege, I love this Australian city and get to walk or cycle along the Yarra River trail and explore the urban alleyways, nooks, crannies, coffee shops, and green spaces. I live in the suburbs, and to get to work in the city, I cross over the south-east freeway where I can peer down across the five-lane car-clogged highway and infamous Melbourne sprawl. The graffiti on the freeway barrier near my home simply says, 'Nature was here'.

If the city of Melbourne is resilient (and importantly this is a question, not a statement), it is critical to ask, for whom, how, in what ways, and to what effect. Resilience, like planning, can mean everything or nothing depending on your perspective. Resilience is a word that feels intuitively good or positive, like freedom or flexibility. Who would not want to be resilient or live in a resilient city? But resilience can mean many different things to different people. Geographer David Harvey writes: 'Freedom is a good place to ride, but ride where?'

The concept of resilient cities was originally predicated on the ability for cities to absorb, recover from, and adapt to crisis. One of the things the resilience lens can encourage is an awareness of the dynamic, complex nature of systems and their environments. This means that adaptability and even transformability are important characteristics of resilient systems. Yet, often the term is more commonly used in a static and prescriptive fashion to reinforce the status quo or defend a conservative agenda. This has led to calls for more transformational understandings of resilience linked to equity and environmental goals.

Resilience has displaced sustainability as the keyword for cities. Emerging strategies for building resilience at all levels from the local to the national primarily reflect efforts to minimize the human impacts of natural disasters, reduce threats to human security posed by the rise of global terrorism, and prepare better for viral epidemics or pandemics. Yet resilience does not have the ethical moorings of sustainability as outlined in the 1987 Brundtland Commission report *Our Common Future*.[15] Its discussion of the need to balance environmental, social, and economic issues, whilst vague, did offer touchpoints for progressive policy and planning. Considerations around intergenerational equity and application of the precautionary principle also laid the foundations for mobilizing community and stakeholder action on climate change.

The resilient city has been embraced across diverse community sectors including defence, business and banks, conservationists, and politicians. Just adding 'community' to 'resilience' does not address the criticism that resilience has been used to serve contrasting political agendas, ranging from neoliberal notions of 'small government' to social democratic notions of a fairer society. Community resilience brings into play questions of equity or opportunity in the social functioning of vulnerable cities. It also poses questions about who might benefit from changes to cities and what might happen to those who feel socially isolated or excluded from collective action in times of turbulence, crisis, and change. Resilience can be co-opted as 'a lens for elites to adopt in coping with the extreme city'.[16]

Instead of questioning and contesting the manufactured insecurities of the extreme city, resilience discourse tends to shunt the responsibility to adapt to hazards onto individuals. Rather than sparking collective solidarity in the face of extreme risk, the idea of resilience tends to disaggregate society ... Resilience has become the dominant jargon for addressing the manifold crises of the extreme city without fundamentally transforming the conditions that give rise to these crises.[17]

We are all invested in seeing cities survive, adapt, and thrive so urban resilience matters. But it is important to be clear about what we mean when we talk about urban resilience. In some cases, there is a need, for example, of certain forms of exclusion to maintain the identity of a community or sub-community within the wider local community. Similarly, the active conservation of local knowledge or traditions may help a local community cope with major disruptions ranging from natural disasters to collapsing global markets. Resistance to change can sometimes be progressive in protecting the form and function of a threatened community, but it can also valorize a static conception of community identity, which is likely to make adaptation and transformation more difficult.

From a strategic perspective, this helps with understanding where we are now, where we have come from and where cities and their communities are going as we move into this strangest and most uncertain of urban futures. The single greatest resilience issue facing the city – and humanity – is climate change or the climate emergency, now and into the future. The Intergovernmental Panel on Climate Change special report on global warming of 1.5 degrees makes unequivocally clear that we are a world racing towards a crisis of our own making; that there is no precedent in history; and that rapid, far-reaching and unprecedented changes are required in all aspects of society. We must act now with everything we have at our disposal.

Urban resilience as equity and solidarity offers an alternative perspective for cities and regions. As urban geographer Brendan Gleeson writes in *Lifeboat Cities,*

Resilience cannot be achieved by shifting the pieces on the board: it requires constant adjustment of the game's rules and tactics. The shift to community economies and the great new enterprise of care are the building blocks of resilience in the next world. Planning must work towards that realization by localizing urban life and nurturing the activities that support the renewal of humans and nature.[18]

Resilience in this sense is about the capacity for urban communities 'to sustain themselves in flourishing relationships with their environment, to cope with catastrophe, and to find ways to continue'.[19] It is fundamentally about connection and commitment to flourishing and care, but in ways that also encompass trauma-scapes and loss. In cities, we embody both the figure of the stray and the friend.

This notion of 'we' builds on Lori Gruen's concept of 'entangled empathy', which embraces both human and non-human encounter. She describes this as a process in which first, we must recognize we are always entangled in multiple relations with others (human and non-human), and that these are often imbalanced. This reflective recognition of the reciprocity of relations is then the basis for taking more responsible interactions, care, and attentiveness to others, with greater consideration of their needs, interests, desires, vulnerabilities, hopes, and sensitivities.[20]

More-than-human cities

Our cities and urban regions are made up of more-than-human actors. The polarization of humans versus non-humans is a telling signifier of the dominance of the human species – one species that is positioned against all other species and non-living entities on the earth and beyond. You are either human or you are part of an incredibly large (yet morally insignificant) amorphous category of the 'non-human' (i.e. the rest of the world). The non-human serves as a 'mirror' for human subjectivity and the struggle over defining the meaning of 'nature'.

The more-than-human project decentres humans as part of a broader entanglement of living and non-living entities. This is a political project where the onus is on 'livingness' as the connection between bodies and worlds. This is the re-animation of a lively earth where humans are no longer the only beings that count.[21] The practice and intention is to destabilize dominant (i.e. Western Cartesian) ideas about knowledge, sociality, materiality, causality, agency, determinism, and ethics, in favour of approaches that are more hybrid, relational and dynamic.[22]

A conceptual sketch of 'the stray', for example, offers a way of shifting human exceptionalism within the context of urban habitats. At core, the stray is homeless, unwanted, an exile, an outsider living in a liminal shadowy space. Commonly associated with domestic companion species (i.e. cats and dogs) gone feral, the term is equally applicable to some individuals of the human species in cities in the age of the Anthropocene: refugees, seasonal workers, illegal immigrants, the homeless, the otherwise unwanted, or the fringe dwellers of the urban realm. Eking out an existence on the margins of civilization, both human and animal strays inhabit an interstitial space that lies somewhere between the 'here' and 'there', 'us' and 'them', and notions of fixity and certainty.

The potential of 'the stray' is addressed in the work of feminist author and academic Barbara Creed who sees the stray as a 'rich and varied concept and lens through which to consider the future of the planet and the lives of all living beings'.[23] She argues for a stray ethics focused on the shared cross-species experiences of urbanization, marginalization, and abandonment. These shared experiences also have the potential to give rise to cross-species recognition, empathy, and resistance. Her point of departure is the unsettling of home and civilization when faced with the precarity, instability, and insecurity of a changing urbanized climate.

The loss of home and habitat applies as much now to citizens of low-lying islands and the victims of migration and exile as to endemic species and neglected urban companion animals. This confluence of experiences radically undermines previous borders and boundaries between species. As Creed observes, 'The human species is in danger of becoming a stray unto itself, a lost species whose ground of being both literally and ethically is shifting so rapidly that darkness engulfs the way ahead.'[24]

The post-human turn

How do we navigate the emerging world of technological modification in the form of genetics, information/smart technology, nanotechnology, artificial intelligence, and virtual worlds? For post-human proponents, the transformation of the human condition via technologies to enhance human intellect and physiology helps create a race of 'superhumans' – smarter, faster, stronger, healthier.

For others, the increasing usage of human enhancement technologies will undermine our very 'human-ness', creating a sub-human or debased human state that blurs the lines between where humans end and machines begin, and vice versa. Whilst the more-than-human approach seeks to decentre the human species, the idea of the post-human has humans deeply embedded at the core, grappling with the prospects of human efficiency and enhancement. The role of technology is important here as the new urban wild.

Technology, while expanding our ability to know in one way, is actually impeding our ability to know in other more complex ways: ways that require: 1) taking responsibility for our own beliefs and 2) working creatively to grasp and reason how information fits together. Put differently information technologies for all their amazing uses are obscuring a simple yet crucial fact: greater knowledge doesn't always bring with it greater understanding.[25]

The 'smart city' lexicon has emerged in an attempt to chart the evolution of an era where information communication technologies (ICTs) and resource-efficient technologies shape the nature and structure of cities: their infrastructure, economic activity, governance, and everyday life. This smart labelling also applies to 'smart people' constituted in and through 'smart' technologies. Digital sociologist Yolande Strengers describes this as 'smart ontology': a vision of technological utopia founded on 'functional securitization and efficiency ideals that work to moderate and control consumer behavior'.[26]

Cities focus on technological innovation as a necessary enabler of smart cities, developed by private companies for public consumption. Yet smart initiatives may implicitly favour affluent parts of cities, an instance of data bias to which big data analytics is vulnerable. Urban geography professor Colin McFarlane writes of a 'dysfunctional' and 'struggling' smart city that is 'splintered', 'unequal', and 'congested'; unable to deliver equitable cities and directed by contested urban imaginaries. This raises questions about equity, access, and distribution. Who benefits from the current normative vision of the smart city and its networked infrastructure technologies?[27]

Dominant notions of the 'smart city' and normative responses to the devastating scale and impact of urban crisis often miss the underlying foundations that structure smart city concepts, ideas of technology. The smart city is a contested idea with multiple possibilities. These are experienced at the personal scale, through lived experiences, and through the political, through social, political, and economic structures of society. In this sense, smart city technologies are seen to extend beyond formal governance and policy processes to expand the possibilities for localized, grassroots community adaptation, mobilization and resistance to threats and disasters. Citizens are now co-creators of the smart city metropolis.

The smart city together with the smart citizen offer new ways to participate and engage with government decision-making processes around crisis and disasters. Technology enables access to information, new communication mediums, and new ways to extend participation into a broader public sphere in eliciting real-time information. It also offers an effective way to engage large numbers of people on difficult public policy issues. Smart technology allows diverse publics the opportunity to 'share democracy'.[28]

There are limits to cyborg citizenship including the reduction of humans to passive participants in democracy, and a lost sense of civic responsibility to community and to ideas.[29] While we all participate in the cyborg cities, a case can be made that the information collection, analysis, and use is highly asymmetric. We load them with wildly different attributes and potential; from those who see them as harbingers of resurgence in local participatory democracy, to those who see them as powerful symbols of state and corporate control.

The smart city extends our way of seeing the urban, whilst simultaneously challenging our very understanding of what it means to be human. In the interplay between machine and organism, the dynamics of nature and culture are reworked. Smart cities are very much places of imagination and invisibility – in that people wherever they are, construct their own cities in their minds.

Like the human-technology-space nexus that complex smart technologies and infrastructures sit within, an equally complex dialectic takes place that forges these new relationships and re-imaginings. Often this is anticipatory and involves the fetishization of the potential for urban system failure precipitated by the destruction of hard and soft critical infrastructure linked so intimately to the survival of capital flow and accumulation.

Reimagining the human-technology-space nexus in this context is about imagining urban futures and their potentialities for new relationships between the city and the public fundamentally changing urban governance, planning, and public participation processes. At the centre of utopian visions for the smart city is a surprisingly conventional view of the smart citizen as a rational utility maximizer, albeit a tech-savvy one, who consciously trades off privacy and convenience in daily practice.

In the era of post-human possibilities and context in which we problematize what it is to be human, are some humans 'more human'? We are all cyborgs now, says critical geographer Donna Haraway, and embody a potent combination of imagination and reality, blurring the boundaries between what is natural and what is artificial. Cyborgs can offer freedom and the possibilities for the reinvention of humankind in terms of gender and race. The cyborg challenges dualistic bodies of situated knowledge and practice, ushering in brave new worlds full of 'potent fusions, dangerous possibilities and fractured identities'.[30]

But cyborgs are hard to see spatially and politically (i.e. the grid control of the planet as a site of hybrid fusion/domination). There are tensions between the foundational figure of the human subject as separate and distinct from other; anti-human celebration; and humanist concerns to affirm and promote human flourishing.[31] This tension creates the potential for opening up new ways of thinking about what being human means. This includes being alert to the ways in which the role of technology is helping to make ourselves 'more than human'. But to what end?

> If we have hope for the future – if we think of ourselves as having such a thing as a future – it is predicated in large part on what we might accomplish through our machines ... And yet the inescapable fact of this moment in history is that we, and these machines of ours, are presiding over a vast project of annihilation, an unprecedented destruction of the world we come to think of as ours. The planet is, we are told, entering a sixth mass extinction: another Fall, another expulsion. It seems very late in the day, in this dismembered world, to be talking about a future.[32]

The sense of 'crisis' when planning and technology fails and our most basic vulnerabilities are exposed can forge new ideas/alternatives about what urban life might be, and what it might become. This changes the nature of humans and non-humans, as well as the technologies the shape and drive the city, making both utopian and dystopian urban futures equally possible.

Urban care and wildness

In the 'mythology of modernism',[33] the city was depicted as a place where nature had been tamed and domesticated into a benign physical environment for primarily human habitation. In the Anthropocene, cities are increasingly understood as both extremely vulnerable and major contributors to a planetary ecological crisis. The human vs. non-human binary is deeply connected to (the wild) settler-colonial oppression of the colonized framed as 'wild'. Such a binary does not exist within Indigenous communities with their spiritual and physical connection to Country.

Average temperatures in Australia and around the globe have risen significantly in the last 50 years, bringing significant changes in the frequency of extreme weather events affecting urban areas, including the increasing frequency, severity, and duration of heat waves and bushfires. In this context, new ways of thinking about the co-existence of humans with each other and with non-humans are necessary. A new conception of cities as 'urban wilds' is emerging, giving rise to existential tensions, fantasies, and deep anxieties. The wild city, as an intellectual concept and as an assemblage of lived practices, puts to test the relationships between the human and non-human, nature and civilization, each other and the 'other'.

This is part of a wider project of dismantling human exceptionalism. Such a project entails moving from a vision – as prejudiced as it is delusional – of humans as gods or an earthly elite, towards embracing our common role in the collective more-than-human earth story. In these lost futures, the wild city is but another failure – the collapse of an existing order, and the rise of a dangerous disorder that cannot be comprehended by humans, let alone controlled by them. But how do we move beyond a hauntology of apocalyptic narratives towards a more constructive conception of the wild city?

The wild city raises a number of questions and challenges with ethical and political implications for urban resilience. There will not be universal approaches or blue-print solutions, but most likely a common starting point that recognizes that not all will be solvable. Any solutions that do evolve will be less certain, with an emphasis on political processes and collective efforts. There will be new forms of relational and representational politics that are inclusive of non-humans in whatever ways are ethical and make sense to apply in different circumstances. This is about embracing knowledge and decision-making within conditions of uncertainty and flexibility. This also means developing new literacies and ethical practices for a changing world.

An ethic of caring-with the wild city focuses on entanglements, not taming, and fusion. This distinction allows for distance alongside responsibility, and for contextualized responses to our urban crisis. Wild-ness can be something to be cherished and honoured in nature, including ourselves as well as denigrated and feared as part of a pervasive cycle of genocide and ecocide. Caring-with is about bearing witness, being present, reconciliation, and commitment to action.

I am reminded to balance a rapidly-shifting pandemic with the timeless lessons of the wild world that awaken deeper attention. Wildness, in this moment, can teach us focus over fear, can teach us humility in the face of natural forces (be they geological or microbial), and can teach us that we are at our best when part of larger systems (be they social or natural) ...

There is wildness now in staying at home.[34]

For most of us, home is in the city – we are as a species inherently urban. The key question is not whether we can care enough for the earth and each other to create the good city, but how to care-with the wild city here and now, with all that we have available. The conditions exist for restoration, but they need to be understood, seeded, and nurtured, and our wounded, darkest places must gently and lovingly be brought to surface to be healed.

If the Angel of History were a wild dog, she'd be a-howling.[35]

Together with care. We must change our cities.

Here and now.

Notes

1 Rabin, R (2020) 'The Coronavirus Outbreak', *The New York Times*, 12 March, accessed on www.nytimes.com/2020/03/12/health/coronavirus-midlife-conditions.html

2 Guterres, A (2020) 'Three Billion in Lockdown as the UN Warns Coronavirus Threatens Humanity', SBS News, 26 March, accessed on www.sbs.com.au/news/three-billion-under-lockdown-as-un-warns-the-coronavirus-threatens-humanity

3 ABC (2020) 'Venice Canals Run Clear as Coronavirus Lockdown Leaves City Free of Tourists', accessed on www.abc.net.au/news/2020-03-19/venice-canals-run-clear-amid-coronavirus-lockdown/12071378

4 Klein, N (2017) 'How Power Profits From Disaster', *The Guardian*, 6 July, accessed on www.theguardian.com/us-news/2017/jul/06/naomi-klein-how-power-profits-from-disaster

5 Ibid., p. 2.

6 Kimmelman, M (2020) 'Can City Life Survive Coronavirus?', in *The New York Times*, 22 March, accessed on www.nytimes.com/2020/03/17/world/europe/coronavirus-city-life.html

7 Ibid., p. 1.

8 Katznelson, G and Wesley-Boyd, J (2018) 'Solitary Confinement: Torture Pure and Simple', *Psychology Today*, 15 January, accessed on www.psychologytoday.com/au/blog/almost-addicted/201801/solitary-confinement-torture-pure-and-simple

9 Kloosterman, R (2016) 'The Dangers of a Tamed City', in Mamadouh, V and van Wagingen, A (eds), *Urban Europe*, University of Amsterdam Press, Amsterdam, p. 191.

10 Sandercock, L (1997) 'The Planner TAMED', *Australian Planner*, 49(4): 285.

11 Ibid., p. 288.

12 Puig de la Bellacasa, M (2017) *Matters of Care: Speculative Ethics in More-Than-human Worlds*, University of Minnesota Press, Minneapolis, p. 1.

13 Tronto, JC and Fisher, B (1990) 'Toward a Feminist Theory of Caring', in Abel, E and Nelson, M (eds), *Circles of Care*, SUNY Press, New York, pp. 36–54.

14 See Power, ER and Williams, MJ (2019) 'Cities of Care: A Platform for Urban Geographical Care Research', *Geography Compass*, and Williams, MJ (2017) 'Care-full Justice in the City', *Antipode*, 49(3): 821–39.
15 Brundtland Report (1986).
16 Dawson, A (2017) *Extreme Cities: The Peril and Promise of Urban Life in the Age of Climate Change*, Verso, London, p. 157.
17 Ibid.
18 Gleeson, B (2010) *Lifeboat Cities*, UNSW Press, Sydney, pp. 188–9.
19 Rose, DB (2004) *Reports from a Wild Country: Ethics for Recolonisation*, University of New South Wales Press, Sydney, p. 7.
20 Gruen, L (2015) *Entangled Empathy: An Alternate Ethic for our Relationships with Animals*, Lantern Books, New York.
21 Whatmore, S (2002) *Hybrid Geographies: Natures Cultures Spaces*, Sage Publications, London; Whatmore, S (2004) 'Humanism's Excess: Some Thoughts of the Post-human/ist Agenda', *Environment and Planning A*, 36(8): pp. 1360–3; Whatmore, S (2006). 'Materialist Returns: Practising Cultural Geography in and for a More-Than-Human world'. *Cultural Geographies* 13(4): 600–9.
22 This is explained in more detail in Houston, D, Hillier, J, MacCallum, D, Steele, W and Byrne, J (2017), 'Make Kin, Not Cities! Multispecies Entanglements and "Becoming-world" in Planning Theory', *Planning Theory*, accessed on http://journals.sagepub.com/doi/full/10.1177/1473095216688042
23 Creed, B (2017) *Stray: Human-animal Ethics in the Anthropocene*, Power Polemics Publications, University of Sydney, Sydney.
24 Ibid., p. 168.
25 Lynch, M (2016) *The Internet of Us: Knowing More and Understanding Less in the Age of Big Data*, Liveright Pub Corporation, London, p. 6.
26 Strengers, Y (2013) *Smart Energy Technologies in Everyday Life: Smart Utopia? Consumption and Public Life*, Palgrave, London, p. 3.
27 McFarlane, C. (2008) Governing the Contaminated City: Infrastructure and Sanitation in Colonial and Post-Colonial Bombay, *International Journal of Urban and Regional Research*, 32(2): 415–35.
28 Ferguson, Michaele L. (2012) *Sharing Democracy*. Oxford University Press, Oxford.
29 Koch, A (2005) Cyber Citizen or Cyborg Citizen: Baudrillard, Political Agency, and the Commons in Virtual Politics, *Journal of Mass Media Ethics* 20(2–3): 159–75.
30 Haraway, D (1984) 'A Cyborg Manifesto', in *Simians, Cyborgs, and Women: The Reinvention of Nature*, Free Association Books, London.
31 Braidotti, R (2013) *The Posthuman*, Polity Press, Cambridge.
32 O'Connell, M (2017) *To Be a Machine: Adventures Among Cyborgs, Utopians, Hackers and the Futurists Solving the Modest Problem of Death*, Granta Publications, London, pp. 6–7.
33 This is a lovely phrase by Ilan Wiesel at the University of Melbourne.
34 Hausdoerffer, J (2020) 'Stay Home, Stay Wild', accessed on www.jhausdoerffer.com/
35 Rose, D (2006) 'What if the Angel of History Were a Dog', *Cultural Studies Review*, 12(1): 67–78.

The journey (Photographer: Scott Blamey)

Index

Page numbers in *italics* denote figures.